AMERICAN COMMAND OF THE SEA
through Carriers, Codes, and the Silent Service:
World War II and Beyond

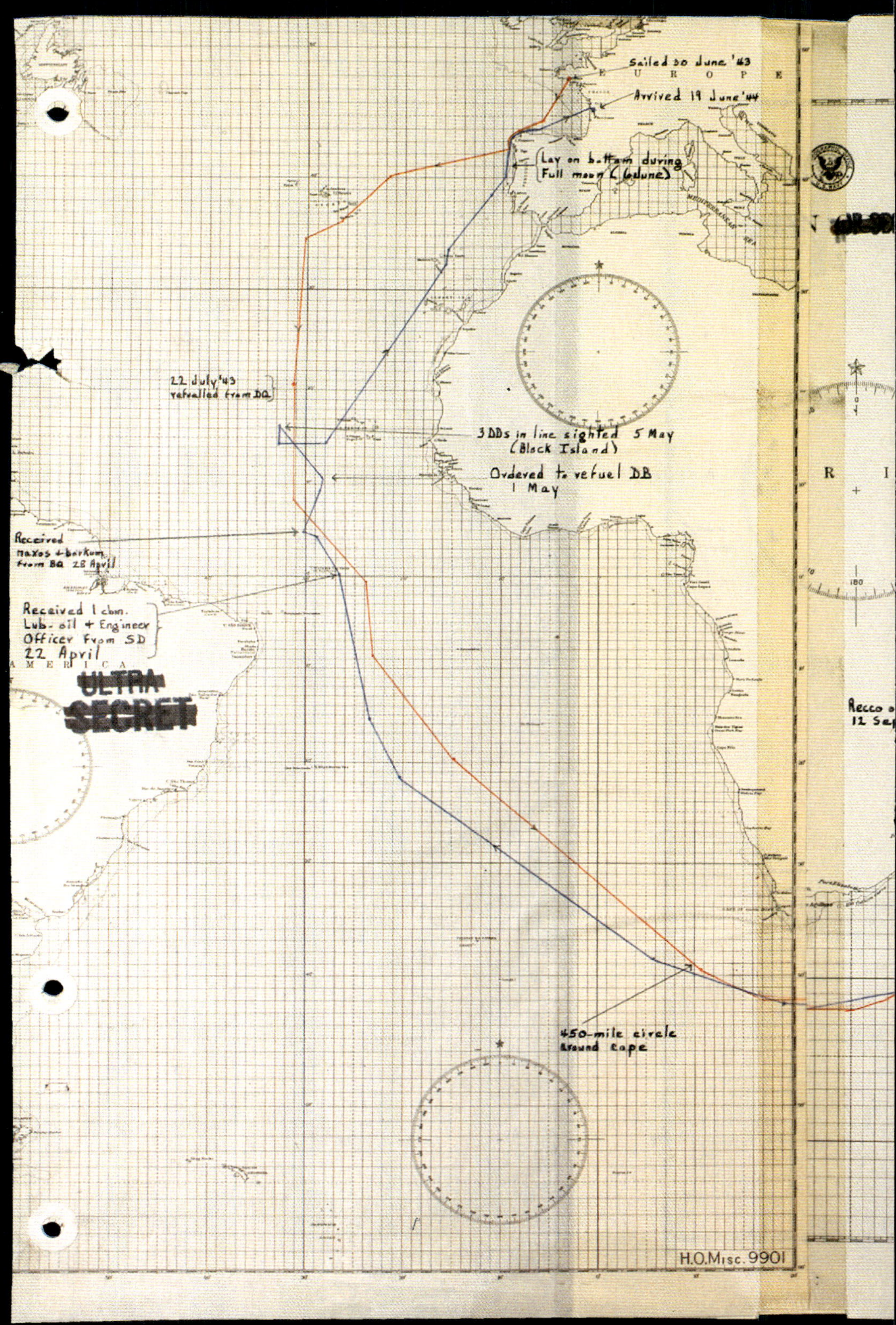

Sailed 30 June '43
E U R O P E
Arrived 19 June '44
Lay on bottom during Full moon (6 June)
MEDITERRANEAN SEA
22 July '43 refuelled from DQ
3 DDs in line sighted 5 May (Block Island)
Ordered to refuel DB 1 May
Received Naxos + Borkum from BQ 28 April
Received 1 cbm. Lub. oil + Engineer Officer from SD 22 April
A M E R I C A
ULTRA SECRET
450-mile circle around Cape
H.O.Misc. 9901

DECLASSIFIED per authorities in NNSC.
Project 953010 Date 8/3/95 by JAD, NARS

ULTRA SECRET

188 (Luedden) cruise to Penang and Return
(30 June 1943 to 19 June 1944)

4 misses on 'candolite type' tanker 6 Oct.
(Elsegundo - 3664 Pan. tkr)

Sank 'Britannia'
9977-t. Nor. tanker
5 Oct.

28 Sept. Convoy course 035
(missed?) six single shots

Chased 10-steamer
Convoy 27 Sept.
(course 215)

Arrived Penang
29 Oct. 43

Sailed Penang
9 Jan. '44

14-20 Oct.
off West Coast India

Spencer
US MV)

8 Sept. refuelled
from Brake

11 March refuelled
from 'Brake'

Brake sunk 12 Mar.

Received cipher from ZY
22 March

Results Homebound Cruise:

A. 20 Jan. Sank 'Fort Buckingham' (7122 Br. MV)
B. 25 Jan. Sank 'Fort La Maune' (7130 Br. MV)
C. 26 Jan. Sank 'Samouri' (7219 Br MV)
D. 26 Jan Sank 'Surada' (5427 Br. MV)
E. 29 Jan. Sank 'Olga E. Embiricos' (4677 Greek MV)
F. 4 Feb. Sank 'Chung Cheng' (7176 chinese MV)
G. 7 Feb. Sank 3 cargo sailers (shelled & rammed)
H. 9 Feb. Sank 'Viva' (3798 Nor. MV)
I. 9 Feb. Sank cargo sailer
J. 10 Feb. miss on tanker
K. 22 Feb. Sank 3 sailing Vessels
L. 14 Feb. sighted Steamer had no torpedoes, no gun

An example of the richness of information gained from signal intelligence. Declassified in August 1995, this ULTRA SECRET map details the year-long voyage of the German submarine *U-188*. Always one jump ahead of Allied attack forces, this U-boat sank some sixteen ships in the Indian Ocean and returned to France on June 19, 1944. (National Archives RG 457.1)

AMERICAN COMMAND OF THE SEA THROUGH CARRIERS, CODES, AND THE SILENT SERVICE:

WORLD WAR II AND BEYOND

by CARL BOYD

THE MARINERS' MUSEUM, NEWPORT NEWS, VIRGINIA

Mariners' Museum publication no. 43

Designed by Raymond Geary

Printed in the United States of America

ISBN 0-917376-43-9

Dedicated to Those Who Have
the Wisdom to Impose Intelligence
on the Battlefield.

Contents

Acknowledgments

One of the joys of writing for publication, even in a relatively brief volume such as this, is the opportunity to acknowledge publicly those who have been involved with the book, for an author's name on the title page represents only part of the story. I feel particularly fortunate to have had the benefit of several good offices and highly professional advice and assistance at The Mariners' Museum. The editing work of Susannah Livingston has improved the worth of this piece immeasurably; similarly, the graphic design work of Raymond Geary and Leann Arndt is refreshingly imaginative. Moreover, if a picture is worth a thousand words, the photographs in this little book turn it into a considerable tome; thus, I am especially grateful for the skillful judgment of those in photographic services: Claudia McFall, John Pemberton, Gregg Vicik, and Aaron Woodcock. It is also a pleasure to acknowledge the assistance of various other individuals and the roles of their sections of the Museum—these include Patty Andresen in collections, Taylor Warren in the library, Priscilla Hauger (exhibition designer), Tom Crew (archivist), and David Baumer (assistant curator). Most expressly, in writing this work I have benefited from observations by Karen Wible, John Hightower, Jürgen Rohwer, and my graduate students David Kohnen and Doug Brooks.

— C. B.

Introduction

The American public has long been aware of the important roles played by submarines and aircraft carriers in World War II. Indeed, in the aftermath of World War I, imaginative military strategists recognized the tremendous potential of these two weapons for future war. Yet the role played by signal intelligence in promoting the effectiveness of submarines and carriers remained murky until the recent declassification of tons of World War II radio communications documents. Now, more than fifty years after the Japanese attack on Pearl Harbor, historians are systematically investigating perhaps the greatest secret of the war—the relationship between the Allies' ability to read enemy codes and ciphers and their ability to bring the war to an end in 1945. Signal intelligence brought greater precision to the war and, in the long run, saved lives and shortened the struggle. It also changed the future of warfare by emphasizing the vital links among intelligence, submarines, and aircraft carriers in the most comprehensive war of the twentieth century.

In the long history of warfare, never has so much information concerning the plans and capacity of the enemy been available to another party as to the Anglo-American powers regarding the Axis coalition during World War II. Allied traditional intelligence operations—commando forays, the work of resistance groups in enemy-occupied territory, spying activities by secret agents, and aerial reconnaissance, for example—were often remarkably sophisticated and successful during the war. Nevertheless, in World War II as today, the *crème de la crème* of clandestine intelligence operations and achievements was in the field of signal communications, the solving of codes and ciphers (cryptanalysis), and the reading of another government's secret communications. Sometimes the Allies were able to decipher and read messages before the rival addressee received them. Never has an adversary had the opportunity to peruse so systematically and thoroughly the most secret communications of an enemy.

1.

2.

3.

5.

6.

Glimpses of the Struggle for Global Command . . .

1. A small watercolor found in the ruins of the Japanese Embassy in Berlin in May 1945. (From the Francis Pickens Miller Collection, George C. Marshall Foundation, Lexington, Virginia)

2. Japanese Ambassador Ōshima and Hitler with German Foreign Minister Ribbentrop (center), Berlin, February 22, 1939. The close relationship between Ōshima and Hitler proved to be a vital source of intelligence once the Japanese Purple cipher system was solved in September 1940 and Ōshima returned to Germany as ambassador in February 1941. (National Archives, 242-JRB-12-75)

3. An American submarine at Pearl Harbor. (Photograph by the author)

4. The submarine escape training tower at Pearl Harbor. (Photograph by the author)

5. A major piece of the Japanese cipher machine *97-shiki Ōbun Injiki* (Alphabetical Typewriter 97) or, as named by Americans, the Purple machine. This was recovered by the United States Army from the Japanese Embassy in Berlin not long after the German surrender in May 1945. (Courtesy of the National Security Agency Museum)

6. The Japanese light aircraft carrier *Ryūjō*. (The Mariners' Museum)

7. Personnel in the Japanese Embassy, including attachés, were extremely popular in wartime Berlin and a good source of intelligence after Japanese ciphers were compromised. In this announcement, a watercolor dated April 21, 1942, the Japanese military attaché, Lieutenant General Banzai, was made an honorary Generalkapitän. (From the Francis Pickens Miller Collection, George C. Marshall Foundation, Lexington, Virginia)

8. The newly constructed Japanese Embassy at 24-27 Tiergartenstrasse, Berlin, was officially opened on January 25, 1943. Heavily bombed during the war but thoroughly rebuilt and expanded in the late 1980s, it is now the Berlin headquarters for a Japanese-German center, Japanisch-Deutsches Zentrum Berlin. (Photograph by the author)

8.

7.

I

BACKGROUND OF SIGNAL INTELLIGENCE

Some background on the development of signal intelligence operations between the two world wars will aid in understanding the enormous effectiveness of U.S. naval submarine and carrier-based air operations after 1941. While these developments were not perfected in time to thwart the Japanese attack on Pearl Harbor, the tedious work of the American cryptologic community in the 1920s and 1930s started to pay off handsomely only a few months after the Japanese attack.

American code-breaking operations had been successful in various wars before the twentieth century. However, code breaking took on national strategic importance because of the experience of Herbert Yardley (1889-1958) and his colleagues in MI-8, the United States Army's new cryptologic section operating in France during World War I. Yardley's reputation as a code expert was further enhanced when he directed the cryptology section of the U.S. delegation to the Paris Peace Conference. In 1919, back in the United States, he was instrumental in establishing the principal cryptanalytic agency of the United States government, the so-called Black Chamber. It was a clandestine, semiofficial organization located in New York City and jointly financed and supported by the State and War departments.

The cryptanalytic work of the small Black Chamber group focused on the reading of foreign diplomatic messages (radio traffic transmitted in Morse code), and results quickly assumed strategic importance. The threat of Japanese naval rivalry with Great Britain and the United States after the scuttling of the German High Seas Fleet in June 1919 became an object of great concern. By the time of the Washington Armament Conference in 1921-1922, Yardley's group was able to read Tokyo's instructions to the Japanese representatives negotiating naval limitations in Washington, D.C. Thus, the U.S. Department of State learned that the Japanese would in the final analysis agree to limit their capital ship fleet to 300,000 tons, compared to approximately 500,000 tons maximum for each of the Anglo-American fleets, that is, a 5:3 ratio. However, the Japanese delegates in Washington were instructed to strive for a far better ratio; failing to obtain Anglo-American agreement, the 5:3 ratio was an acceptable bottom line. The American delegation insisted on the 5:3 ratio from the outset, never budging in weeks of talks until the Japanese eventually agreed. Thus, relative big-ship strengths among the major powers were fixed for ten years by international agreement, and the strategic ramifications were clear.

The United States Navy was also involved in code breaking in the 1920s. In 1925 the navy's Communications Division's Code and Signal Section (later called OP-20-G) began to develop a system of cryptanalytic and traffic analysis centers, intercept stations, and radio direction finders. Japanese operational naval codes and ciphers were a chief target.

The navy emphasized the training of serving intelligence officers, while the United States Army relied more heavily on civilian personnel for the difficult and expensive work of cryptography. Cooperation between the two services was intermittent and often difficult, but with signs of the coming of another war in which the United States might be a belligerent, collaboration in communications intelligence replaced much of the suspicion and jealousy between the services. For example, in 1940 and 1941 the army's Signal Intelligence Service (SIS) and the navy's counterpart, OP-20-G, had a special agreement for work on Japanese diplomatic traffic. The army processed all messages of an even date and the navy all messages of an odd date, with full exchange of technical data and results. A few months after the attack on Pearl Harbor, however, the navy became so taxed by the demands for additional study of various Japanese navy cryptographic systems that it relinquished (in agreement with the Federal Bureau of Investigation and the army) its involvement with "Purple," the American name for the cipher machine that the Japanese called *97-shiki Ōbun Injiki* (Alphabetical Typewriter 97 or Cipher Machine, Type B). In personal communication with this author, key wartime cryptanalyst Frank B. Rowlett, who later received U.S. congressional and presidential as well as British awards and declarations for his work, noted that the army

Part of the Japanese Purple machine found at the Japanese Embassy in Berlin, May 1945. (Courtesy of the National Security Agency. Photograph by The Mariners' Museum.)

> felt that the intelligence from the Japanese diplomatic messages, particularly those exchanged between Tokyo and Berlin, Rome, and Moscow, would be of vital importance in the prosecution of the war. Accordingly, the decision was made by the Army to expand its effort on the Japanese diplomatic messages, to insure that all Japanese diplomatic intercepts could be promptly processed and the resulting information provided to U.S. intelligence agencies. This arrangement continued until the Japanese surrendered.

Purple—MAGIC, Enigma—ULTRA

The army's SIS broke into Purple, by far the most difficult of Japanese cryptographic systems. Introduced in 1938, Purple remained largely secure until late 1940, when SIS head cryptanalyst William F. Friedman and Frank Rowlett, who worked primarily on the Japanese diplomatic intercepts as one of the earliest members of the SIS staff, were largely responsible for the solution. In the 1930s Friedman often referred to his dedicated staff of cryptanalysts as "magicians," and it was probably his use of this appellation that later gave rise to the cover name MAGIC.

For a "profound contribution to the security of the United States," cryptanalyst Frank B. Rowlett (between his wife, Edith Rowlett, and President Lyndon Johnson) received the National Security Medal from the president on March 2, 1966. The citation mysteriously added that Rowlett had applied his "creative energy to a wide range of the most complex technical and technological problems." (Courtesy of Henry F. Schorreck)

The term MAGIC was used by Americans to denote intelligence obtained from breaking the Japanese high-grade wireless enciphered diplomatic messages. It also came to be a cover name for all intelligence produced by the solution of foreign codes and ciphers. However, distinct nomenclature was not always adhered to during the war, especially after 1943, when American intelligence specialists were systematically given access to ULTRA, the name the British gave to information obtained from breaking German wireless traffic enciphered on the Enigma machine. In time, the term "Japanese ULTRA" was commonly used by Americans for information obtained from reading Japanese navy, army, and air cryptologic systems.

A German four-wheel Enigma machine. (Courtesy of the National Security Agency. Photograph by The Mariners' Museum.)

The number of intercepted Japanese cipher messages increased dramatically during the war. The enormous flood of communications can be estimated by the number of messages in Purple sent personally by the Japanese ambassador in Berlin to the Foreign Ministry in Tokyo (excluding many more—some in Purple, some using other cipher systems—sent by the embassy's attachés and secretaries). There were approximately 75 messages in 1941, 100 in 1942, 400 in 1943, 600 in 1944, and 300 during the first four months of 1945, that is, until the German surrender. Message length varied from the equivalent of one to thirty pages of typed, single-spaced text. Adding to the total were Tokyo's responses and hundreds of thousands of other enemy messages, often containing detailed operational and tactical information, and employing many different cipher systems. U.S. government cryptographic operations struggled to keep pace, and some recorded intercepts were not deciphered and translated until months or even years later.

Security

The enormous volume of enemy intercepts increased the risk of leaks. There was great concern at the highest levels of the U.S. wartime government for the safeguarding of the MAGIC and ULTRA secrets. Nevertheless, the British sometimes felt that American security was not stringent enough. The two Allied governments were unable to "agree to exchange completely all information concerning the detection, identification and interception of signals from, and the solution of codes and ciphers used by . . . the Axis powers" until the agreement between the U.S. War Department and the British Government Code and Cipher School (GC & CS) was concluded on May 17, 1943. The problem was how to edit special intelligence and then distribute it speedily to strategic managers of the war.

The War Department was primarily responsible for handling and disseminating special signal intelligence directly to the President of the United States and to the heads of certain other executive departments. Special Branch, Military Intelligence Service (MIS) in the Pentagon compiled daily summaries in which the most important information was gleaned from each day's batch of intercepted messages. At the outset, these messages in Morse code were deciphered and translated a short distance away at SIS, Arlington Hall Station, Virginia. Producing finished intelligence from raw information was like separating the wheat from the chaff, claimed United States Army Chief of Staff George C. Marshall as he sought to make the essential information readily available to those who needed to know, most of them in Washington, D.C. At the same time, he sought not to overwhelm them with the tremendous mass of daily intercepts. Marshall himself usually saw only the summaries, although occasionally when pursuing special points he would have SIS send him the originals of particular intercepted messages. British Prime Minister Winston Churchill, while in Washington, D.C., for wartime conferences with the president, would also sometimes

Arlington Hall Station, formerly Arlington Hall Junior College for Girls in Virginia, was headquarters for the army's Signal Intelligence Service beginning in the spring of 1942. (Courtesy of United States Army INSCOM)

ask to see the originals of particular intercepts. The summaries were not intended to offer editorial comment beyond the minimum necessary to identify a person, place, or situation with an appropriate backdrop or reference.

Knowledge of the MAGIC and ULTRA secrets was restricted to a very small circle early in the war, and the extreme security measures required for handling these secrets necessarily kept many theater and field commanders in the dark about special signal intelligence. General Dwight D. Eisenhower, for example, did not learn about ULTRA until late June 1942, when Churchill, very privately and with much personal delight (for the prime minister was a devotee to signal intelligence and its enormous importance), enlightened the newly appointed United States Army commander of the European theater of operations. Getting the secrets into the hands of appropriate field commanders obviously increased the risk of compromise unless a thoroughly secure dissemination system could be devised.

Dissemination Arrangements

The need for dissemination of special signal intelligence to United States Army field commands did not become acute until 1943. In March, SIS made its first entry into the mainline Japanese military systems. Earlier, however, the United States Navy had a direct cipher channel to Pearl Harbor, with an extension to the commander of the Seventh Fleet in Brisbane. General Douglas MacArthur also had his own cryptanalytic organization in Australia, with special channels of communication to Arlington Hall Station and to GC & CS at Bletchley Park outside London. Throughout the North African campaign (September 1940–May 1943), German military ULTRA produced by Bletchley Park (not by Arlington Hall) was disseminated by British Special Liaison Units (SLUs) to key American officers in accord with British security practices. However, American intelligence officers in Washington did not receive this service until 1943.

The 1943 Anglo-American agreement on special intelligence stipulated that both governments disseminate MAGIC and ULTRA secrets to their own operational commands. Thus, in the summer of 1943 the American Special Security Officer (SSO) system, patterned after the British SLU organization of 1940, was devised for the dissemination of communications intelligence to the commanders at the battle fronts.

SSOs, under the operational command of the Assistant Chief of Staff, Intelligence (G-2) in Washington, D.C., were carefully recruited. The first group of twenty officers began training in July 1943 and was sent overseas and attached to theater headquarters in September. Each SSO carried with him his own set of cryptographic equipment for enciphering and deciphering messages. A special pouch service was instituted, and materials such as the MAGIC summaries were always sent in a TOP SECRET pouch. Both radio cipher and pouch communications were sent directly and only to the SSO. The SSO did the actual deciphering himself and personally showed the messages to the theater commander and certain staff officers who were authorized and designated by authorities in Washington, D.C., for receipt of special intelligence. Security regulations did not permit theater commands to keep SSO messages; rather, the SSO was responsible for custody until the messages were destroyed. Although the SSO system was not perhaps as masterful as the more highly centralized British SLU organization, the system proved safe and generally quite effective. (SSOs found that work with MacArthur's Southwest Pacific command was often extremely difficult, but then, officials in Washington, from President Roosevelt down, sometimes found it hard to influence and work with MacArthur.) Much special signal intelligence would have lost its value had it not been passed on swiftly and safely to the commanders who used it in action.

For the United States Navy fleets at sea, the SSO system was hardly practical; however, the navy collaborated with the British a year before the United States Army established a liaison. Secure communication channels were most often used to transmit operational intelligence directly to the fighting ships, especially from the field processing units at Pearl Harbor and Melbourne, Australia. The flow of naval signal intelligence from these units was coordinated in Washington, D.C. By 1945 naval signal intelligence centers at Washington and Pearl Harbor were transmitting up to a million words daily.

Significance of Special Intelligence

MAGIC and ULTRA secrets contributed significantly to the Allies' ability to conclude the war in 1945. Special intelligence was crucial in numerous aspects of the war at sea, particularly in the vast Pacific, where a premium was placed on advance information about the enemy's intentions. By reading the enemy's messages, the Allies often gained the time needed to meet the challenge with precision from great distances. Some examples follow of instances in which this intelligence made a difference in the Pacific Ocean:

United States Navy Submarine Campaign against Japan

ULTRA provided often precise information on the location and composition of Japanese merchant ship convoys and warship forces—information that allowed American submarines to be used with maximum efficiency. At the peak of United States Navy submarine strength, there were only 169 fleet-type submarines in operation. With only 1.6 percent of U.S. naval personnel, the submarine force was able to sink about 55 percent of Japanese merchantmen (1,178 ships) and about 20 percent of the Imperial warships (214 vessels) lost in attacks by all U.S. forces. ULTRA also enabled the Allies to track the progress of the campaign and assess the overall damage to the Japanese economy.

Battle of Midway

Early information on Japanese operational plans allowed U.S. carrier forces, assisted by land-based air power, to set up an ambush of greatly superior Japanese carrier forces in

June 1942. This resulted in the loss of four Japanese carriers and a portion of their highly trained air crews. The lost ships and crews could not be replaced by the Japanese. A Japanese diversion in the Aleutians, recognized as such through communications intelligence, did not distract U.S. forces from the main effort to prevent the Japanese invasion of Midway.

Battle of the Bismarck Sea

In March 1943, data regarding Japanese locations and operational plans provided via cryptologic analysis integrated with more traditional intelligence allowed Allied air power to sink most of a Japanese transport convoy sent from Rabaul, New Britain, to reinforce Japanese forces at Lae, New Guinea. Eight Japanese transport ships and four destroyers were sunk; some three thousand Japanese troops were lost. Thus, by the time Lae fell in September, Japanese defenses in New Britain-New Guinea were in shambles.

Hollandia Invasion

MacArthur was able to use ULTRA effectively during the April 22, 1944, invasion, bypassing a strong Japanese garrison at Hansa Bay, New Guinea, severing its supply line, and advancing his timetable of conquest.

Yanagi Operations

The Germans and Japanese exchanged critical materials and technology by using first surface ships and later submarines as blockade runners. Information from ULTRA about these Yanagi operations enabled Allied forces to attack these vessels with precision in the vastness of the Indian Ocean and elsewhere during their long east-west voyages. For example, an ULTRA message of June 25, 1944, described the sinking of the Japanese submarine *I-52* west of the Cape Verde Islands in the Atlantic. Near midnight on June 24, aircraft from the USS *Bogue* (CVE-9) dropped flares, sonar buoys, and an acoustic torpedo, the Mark-24 mine known also as Fido, on a "very large sub." The submarine submerged, bombs exploded "followed by breaking up sounds." Bales of crude rubber, a Japanese sandal, fragments of silk, "human flesh and mahogany [were] recovered from large oil slick."

Yamamoto Shoot Down

On April 13, 1943, signal intelligence provided Allied planners with the precise arrangements and timing of an impending inspection flight by Admiral Isoroku Yamamoto, commander in chief of Japan's Combined Fleet. The American deciphering of this initial message was made easier because it was obtained by several wide-ranging Allied radio intercept stations. There appeared to be an opportunity to ambush Yamamoto's plane. After conferring with Secretary of the Navy Frank Knox, who consulted President Roosevelt, Admiral Chester W. Nimitz, commander in chief of the Pacific Fleet, authorized Admiral William H. Halsey's forces to shoot down Admiral Yamamoto's plane. On April 18, P-38s flew from Henderson Field on Guadalcanal to intercept Yamamoto's plane over Bougainville. They flew a circuitous course out at sea for some 420 miles and at an altitude of 50 feet as added insurance against being spotted by Japanese coast watchers and radar. With a window for attack of less than five minutes, American fliers shot down and killed Japan's most capable naval leader; his successors proved much less capable as Combined Fleet commanders.

Admiral Isoroku Yamamoto, commander in chief of Japan's Combined Fleet. (Naval Historical Center NHC-PB-NH 63430)

The Defeat of German U-boats

The most significant contribution of signal intelligence in the Atlantic was the destruction of the U-boat force. Britain's survival depended on secure supply lines. ULTRA often enabled convoys en route to Great Britain and the Soviet Union to evade U-boat patrol lines, and Allied naval forces, relying heavily on signal intelligence, were eventually able to destroy the vast German U-boat fleet. Out of 842 U-boats that were assigned to battle duty, 783 (93 percent) were wiped out. Of a total enlistment of about 39,000 U-boat sailors, 28,000 were killed and 5,000 taken prisoner.

Admiral Chester W. Nimitz, commander in chief of the United States Navy Pacific Fleet. (MacArthur Archives)

In order to maintain the U-boat threat against North Atlantic supply routes and to threaten more distant vital regions—the East Coast of the U.S., the Gulf of Mexico, the South Atlantic, and the Indian Ocean—the Germans converted relatively ineffective minelayer U-boats to refueling and resupplying submarines. In 1943, however, work started on the U-tanker, a submarine specifically designed as a refueling craft; thus, a situation was created in which each combat U-boat could double its range and nearly double its patrol time. In all, eighteen U-tankers became operational before the end of the war in Europe in May 1945, and all but two, *U-219* and *U-234*, were sunk. Usually U-tankers were specifically targeted with the aid of ULTRA, as their destruction suddenly became a top priority of the Allies. In many instances the trapdoor was not sprung until several fuel-hungry combat U-boats were converging on a U-tanker or were actually tied up, refueling, and particularly vulnerable to sudden attack.

A World War II depth-charge attack against a submerged submarine. (The Mariners' Museum PU 29)

Right: A German three-wheel Enigma machine in a U-boat during World War II. (Bundesarchiv MW 4222 2A)

Below: The *U-172* arriving at Lorient, France, July 20, 1942. (Bundesarchiv MW 4392 3)

Top: The *I-30* sailing out of Lorient, France, on August 21, 1942, to return to East Asian waters with a prize cargo of German technical equipment. On October 13, 1942, this submarine struck a British mine at Singapore. Much of the valued cargo and thirteen members of the 100-man crew were lost. (Bundesarchiv MW 5062 23)

Left: Japanese sailors from the *I-30* watching the arrival of a U-boat at Lorient, France, August 1942. (Bundesarchiv MW 4426 14A)

Above: Japanese and German sailors talking at Lorient, France, August 1942. (Bundesarchiv MW 4428 3)

Other Examples of the Effectiveness of ULTRA and MAGIC

ULTRA intelligence was also valuable in many other aspects of the war against Germany and Italy. For example, ULTRA was important in the planning of strategic bombing operations, particularly against Germany's oil industry and transportation system, and served as a barometer for measuring the effectiveness of the bombing. It contributed to Anglo-American success in North Africa and it revealed much information about V-2 rocket sites in Germany and German-occupied territory. MAGIC and ULTRA messages frequently offered a good reading of economic conditions inside Axis countries, and MAGIC frequently provided Anglo-American strategists with specific exhibits of conditions on the crucial German-Soviet front. Much of the importance of special intelligence also lay in revealing the whole picture of "the other side of the hill." MAGIC, in particular, often disclosed the states of mind, attitudes, and intentions of Axis leaders, some of which were already partially revealed through more traditional intelligence sources. Nevertheless, signal intelligence tended to provide extremely up-to-date information. For example, on the eve of the landings at Normandy, by far the largest and most complex amphibious operation ever undertaken, one question continued to haunt Eisenhower and his lieutenants: How would Adolf Hitler's forces react to the invasion? MAGIC revealed that Allied deception operations to disguise the actual site of the forthcoming landings were effective among most members of Hitler's upper echelons, including Hitler himself. Thus, Eisenhower learned of Hitler's attitudes and stubborn beliefs about the coming invasion before it was too late to take advantage of the Führer's errors.

There are many variables to be considered when studying World War II, but there can be no doubt that the Allied "reading of the enemy's mail" helped to shorten the war by perhaps two years, reduce the loss of life, and make inevitable an eventual Allied victory. □

II

BACKGROUND OF THE UNITED STATES NAVY SUBMARINE FORCE

The development of the "silent service," the United States Navy submarine force, moved ahead dramatically in the 1920s. Submarines escaped both abolition and restriction in the Naval Limitation Treaty resulting from the Washington Conference in 1922. However, with the ten-year building restriction on capital ships and the agreement not to build new naval bases or extend old ones (namely Guam and Manila, which were not to be fortified), the navy's objective shifted from emphasis on maintaining a force of small, slow coastal and harbor defense submarines to a push to develop larger and faster submarines.

Characteristics of American submarines were dictated in large part by the environment in which the boats were obligated to operate, and the vastness of the Pacific Ocean was no minor consideration in shaping the equipment of the silent service. The Pacific Ocean is more than twice the size of the Atlantic Ocean, and distances between major American naval facilities in the Pacific and key overseas naval installations are much greater. For example, there are approximately 3,400 nautical miles between Norfolk, Virginia, and Portsmouth, England, whereas there are 2,278 nautical miles between San Diego and Pearl Harbor, and beyond Hawaii—where the war eventually took place—there are nearly 4,800 miles to Manila, 3,400 miles to Yokosuka, and 6,100 miles to Singapore. Moreover, it appeared in the interwar period that distant Japan was more likely to become a naval adversary of the United States than any major European naval power.

U.S. naval advocates sought sizable submarines with higher speed, greater endurance, improved reliability, and more powerful weapons systems. Such submarines, most notably in Pacific Ocean operations, could serve as scouts and pickets and could better accompany the battleships of the day, the *Nevada*, *Pennsylvania*, *New Mexico*, *Tennessee*, and *Maryland* classes. Nevertheless, the last of fifty-one old S-boats, considered inferior to World War I German U-boats, was launched in 1924 and delivered to the United States Navy the following year. The best design of these American S-boats had a top speed of 15 knots, a displacement of 876 tons surfaced, a length of 231 feet, four 21-inch torpedo tubes with twelve torpedoes, one 4-inch/50-caliber deck gun, and a complement of thirty-eight. Designed diving depth was only 200 feet. The United States Navy realized that if war came and it was denied naval facilities in the western Pacific, the small S-boats with a range of about 3,000 nautical miles at 6.5 knots surfaced were incapable of carrying out extensive western patrols while operating out of Pearl Harbor.

The fleet-type submarine started to dominate the American silent service. Follow-

Top: The USS *Oklahoma* (BB-37), completed in 1916, was one of two battleships of the *Nevada* class. Displacement was 27,600 tons, top speed was 20.5 knots. (The Mariners' Museum, Ted Stone Collection)

Above: The USS *Arizona* (BB-39), a *Pennsylvania* class battleship, was completed in 1916. Displacement was 31,400 tons, top speed was 21 knots. (The Mariners' Museum, Ted Stone Collection PN 6032)

ing their introduction in 1924, the large fleet submarines evolved through their heyday in the Pacific (1943–1945) and into the 1970s, when their last representatives retired from the U.S. fleet. The *Barracuda* class (*V1*) was foremost when launched in July 1924. Its top surface speed was 18.7 knots, range was 6,000 nautical miles at 11 knots surfaced, displacement was 2,119 tons surfaced, and length was 325 feet. It had six 21-inch torpedo tubes with twenty torpedoes, one 5-inch/51-caliber deck gun, and a complement of eighty-five. Like the S-boats, the original V-boats were designed to dive to 200 feet.

Top: Postcard showing the Japanese battleship *Fusō*, completed in 1915. Displacement was 30,600 tons, top speed was 22.5 knots. (The Mariners' Museum)

Above: Postcard showing the Japanese battleship *Hyūga*, completed in 1918. Displacement was 31,260 tons, top speed was 23 knots. (The Mariners' Museum)

Top: Postcard showing the Japanese battleship *Mutsu*, completed in 1920. Displacement was 33,800 tons, top speed was 26.5 knots. (The Mariners' Museum)

Above: One of the largest of United States Navy submarines in the interwar period, the USS *Nautilus* (SS-168) is seen here on July 1, 1930, as the N2. The photograph was taken from the N1, the USS *Narwhal* (SS-167). These submarines each carried two 6-inch, 53-caliber deck guns. (The Mariners' Museum, Ted Stone Collection)

Modification and refinement of various classes of fleet submarines took place in the late 1920s and throughout the 1930s. Not infrequently until about 1933, American submarines used reliable German diesel engines, particularly special licensed MAN diesels (*Maschinenfabrik-Augsburg-Nürnberg*). Thereafter, new fleet submarines were built most often with American diesel engines manufactured by Fairbanks-Morse or General Motors. With the development of better, long-range, more habitable submarines (the first submarine air-conditioning system was installed in 1935), a new role for United States Navy submarines started to take shape among naval strategists.

Rather than tying submarines directly to battle fleet support roles, strategists placed more emphasis on the idea of independent submarine patrols, offensive operations against enemy ships, and intelligence-gathering missions. This gradual change in the fleet submarine's capability and role starting in the mid-1930s seemed propitious in the wake of the damage and destruction of the Pearl Harbor battle fleet in December 1941. Indeed, unrestricted submarine warfare, important especially to submarines on independent patrols, was declared six hours after the surprise attack. Lingering remnants of prewar doctrine were abandoned and overwhelmed by reality: no longer was there emphasis on a decisive fleet engagement with submarine support. Orders were issued from Washington lifting all restrictions on submarine warfare against Japanese warships and merchantmen alike. Yet at the outset of the Pacific War the effectiveness of the inexperienced United States Navy submarine force paled in comparison with the German U-boat command. Fifteen American submarines sank fifteen ships in Japanese waters in the first three months of 1942; during the same period eleven U-boats sank at least 204 ships in U.S. waters—more than 1,000,000 tons of shipping.

By 1942 the standard-bearer *Balao* class was launched, the most numerous of any single class of United States Navy submarine. The USS *Balao* (SS-285) had a top surface speed of 20.25 knots, a range of 11,000 nautical miles at 10 knots surfaced, a displacement of 1,525 tons surfaced, a length of 311 feet, ten 21-inch torpedo tubes with twenty-four torpedoes, one 3-inch/50-caliber deck gun, and a complement of eighty. A key feature of the *Balao* class was its designed diving depth of 400 feet, 100 feet greater than its immediate predecessor. That increase in operating depth was one of the best-kept secrets of the war, and such security no doubt prevented the loss of many American submariners. Japanese destroyers continued in many instances to set their depth-charge detonation devices at more shallow depths; thus, the *Balao* class boats often avoided the full blast of a perhaps otherwise fatal depth-charging. Nearly 120 submarines of this class were built during the war, some of them in as little as six months from the date the keel was laid until the submarine was fully commissioned. Wartime modifications particularly influenced deck armament; 20- and 40-millimeter light anti-aircraft guns were mounted on a "cigarette deck" fore and aft and some boats were fitted with 4-inch/50-caliber or 5-inch/25-caliber deck guns.

Top: The after engine room of the USS *Pickerel* (SS-524). Seen are two of the submarine's four 1,600-horsepower Fairbanks-Morse diesel engines. The temperature could easily reach 130 degrees in the two engine rooms when the hot engines were suddenly shut down and the submarine started to dive. (Photograph by the author)

Above: Artist's depiction of an American submarine sinking a Japanese warship during World War II. (The Mariners' Museum LP 3000)

Top: Attack of the USS *Barb* (SS-220). (The Mariners' Museum LN 45)

Above: The German submarine *U-402*, October 1942. (Bundesarchiv MW 6853 37)

Opposite (top): The longitudinal section of a United States Navy World War II submarine. (The Mariners' Museum)

Opposite (bottom): The USS *Mingo* (SS-261) was launched on November 30, 1942. (The Mariners' Museum, Ted Stone Collection)

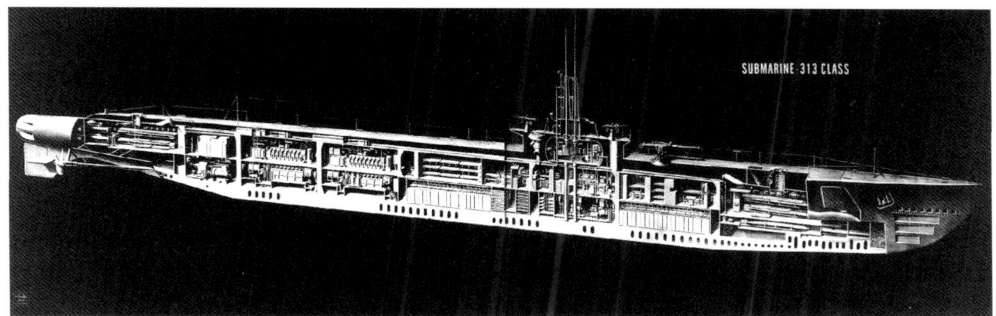
SUBMARINE 313 CLASS

Technological Developments for Precision Warfare

Improved communication systems sought to overcome distances at sea. By 1923 submarine radios were able to make surface Morse code transmissions up to 300 nautical miles. By the end of the decade, a distance of 500 miles, depending on a submarine's position and atmospheric conditions, was commonly attainable. During World War II, United States Navy submarines on patrol in the western Pacific, though normally operating under radio silence, did have the capability to transmit very important messages back to headquarters at Brisbane, Australia, or Pearl Harbor. Late in the war a whip antenna was developed for submarines. When extended, it enabled a submarine to transmit messages while running with decks awash. Also late in the war, short-range direct voice communication between submarines (including those in wolf packs) and surface ships, land units, and aircraft was effective. Today, much more sophisticated underwater voice communication equipment is used for communicating between United States Navy submarines and surface ships. Examples are the voice system called the AN/WQC2 and the underwater coded communication system called the AN/WQC6, which employs a cipher key.

It was extremely important for submarines on patrol to be able to receive instructions or operational reports whether they were submerged or surfaced. Receiving radio messages in a submerged submarine was, of course, more difficult, but by 1930 experiments revealed that very low frequency radio waves could be picked up by a grounded loop antenna of a submerged submarine. Eventually, wartime submarines were fitted with such special antennas mounted near the top of the periscope supports, and reception was generally good while a submarine was running submerged at periscope depth.

Radar also brought greater precision to submarine operations in the war in the Pacific. In 1940, the USS *Gar* (SS-206) was fitted with an omnidirectional aircraft warning set known as SD. It became standard equipment by 1942, but it was sadly primitive: it merely indicated that an aircraft was nearby; its emissions enabled Japanese aircraft to home in on the submarine target; and it was triggered even by aircraft not flying toward a surfaced submarine. Later in 1942, the USS *Haddock* (SS-231) was fitted with the much more sophisticated SJ sensor, a surface-search radar. Bearing, course, and speed of a target could often be determined even during night attacks, but range was limited. A surface ship radar mast some 100 feet above the waterline could detect shipping at ranges around 15 miles; however, the low silhouette of the submarine reduced reliable ranges to rarely more than 7 nautical miles. In late 1943, Identification of Friend or Foe (IFF) equipment was installed for the first time on the USS *Angler* (SS-240); thereafter, submarines were given more protection from "friendly fire." (At least two American submarines were sunk by friendly fire during the war.) By 1944, Japanese submarines were using radar, but American submarines were at the same time being equipped with intercept and countermeasures (ECM) sets. Thus, they could dive long before being detected by Japanese submarines, and the ECM emitted no telltale signal of its own.

In November 1943 one American submarine—the USS *Corvina* (SS-226)—was sunk by a Japanese submarine, but at least seventeen Japanese submarines were sunk by U.S. submarines during the war: four in 1942, one in 1943, six in 1944, and six in 1945.

Sonar equipment, particularly supersonic echo-ranging and listening sonar, was standard in U.S. submarines in the interwar period, but the first fully integrated system, the WDA, was placed in service in early 1941. The sound heads for the WDA were usually mounted on a retractable shaft that could be lowered beyond the bottom of the hull from inside the forward torpedo room. A year later JP sonar equipment was introduced. With a T-shaped hydrophone mounted on deck over the forward torpedo room and trained manually from below, this passive listening sonar employed sonic frequencies as the operator listened through headphones and observed a dial indicator to determine the bearing of a target. Various improvements were also made on sonar equipment to facilitate detection of torpedoes and monitoring of other noises. In 1944 a frequency modulated (FM) sonar was particularly successful when it produced a characteristic ringing echo from mines and similar underwater objects. Yet many submarine casualties were suffered because the effectiveness of all World War II sonar equipment was often sharply reduced by adverse water conditions. The United States Navy lost fifty-two submarines during the war from all causes: one in 1941, seven in 1942, seventeen in 1943, nineteen in 1944, and eight in 1945. However, only forty-one U.S. submarine losses were due directly to Japanese action, including passive means such as mines. There were a total of 248 United States Navy fleet submarines in commission during the war years. About 3,500 submariners died out of some 16,000 who actually made war patrols. This casualty rate of nearly 22 percent was the highest of any branch of the United States armed forces in World War II.

ULTRA and the Silent Service

A thoroughly reliable communication system was essential if American submarines were to use ULTRA information effectively. ULTRA brought more precision to the war than any other wartime innovation. Yet code breakers were obsessed with the security of signal intelligence, and dissemination of ULTRA at sea was extremely limited, especially early in the war. Systematic cooperation with the silent service took more than a year to develop after the first three United States Navy submarines left Pearl Harbor within a week of the attack to patrol Japanese home waters. These submarines were the USS *Gudgeon* (SS-211), *Pollack* (SS-180), and *Plunger* (SS-179). OP-20-G in Washington issued the strictest guidelines for the use of signal intelligence, stating that it could be released only if important strategic objectives or major enemy targets were at stake. In effect these severe restrictions usually precluded ULTRA-based attacks by independent submarines in distant enemy waters. It was assumed that there was too much danger of capture and compromise of the ULTRA secret from submarines in Japanese home waters.

However, in February 1942 there arose an opportunity for a submarine to strike at a major enemy target. The Japanese port director at Truk transmitted a message concerning the forthcoming sailing of an aircraft carrier. This intercepted information was passed to the submarine force at Pearl Harbor, although the source of the intelligence was not revealed to the silent service. In a secret coded radio message, submarine headquarters diverted the USS *Grayling* (SS-209), the only submarine in position for possible interception of the Japanese carrier. However, it arrived off Truk too late to make an attack, and the submerged *Grayling* could only watch with anguish as the carrier sailed out of harbor and over the horizon. Nevertheless, the precedent was established. Strategists recognized the potential to employ signal intelligence more effectively by giving information to the silent service. However, a fully reliable ULTRA dissemination system would not be worked out until early 1943.

A better opportunity for ULTRA and the silent service developed in May 1942. A deciphered Japanese message revealed that the escort carrier *Taiyō*, converted from the 19,000-ton passenger liner *Kasuga Maru*, would soon arrive in Kwajalein harbor. This time submarine headquarters was given ample warning and the USS *Gato* (SS-212) was waiting. Five torpedoes were fired under almost ideal conditions, but they all missed the target. Code breakers at Pearl Harbor wondered aloud if passing ULTRA to submariners, and thus risking compromise, was justified if submarines could not hit their targets. However, this incident helped to confirm defects of United States Navy torpedoes.

The American submarine force had long been plagued by faulty torpedoes. (At least two American submarines were sunk by circular runs of their own torpedoes during the war. Their torpedoes obviously had defective rudder mechanisms.) Deciphered Japanese reports of U.S. submarine attacks on their ships sometimes revealed that American torpedoes ran harmlessly under the target (where torpedoes with magnetic exploders were intended to explode), or scored direct hits without exploding, or exploded prematurely before reaching the target. Sometimes captured Japanese sailors revealed that their ships had been torpedoed *twice* by American submarines, once harmlessly when the torpedoes failed to explode and the second time when the torpedoes were functional. In spite of such overwhelming evidence, the Naval Torpedo Station at Newport, Rhode Island, operating under the Bureau of Ordnance of the Department of the Navy, continued to maintain, sometimes even after additional elaborate tests, that the torpedo depth control mechanism, the contact exploder, and the magnetic exploder were all accurate and fully reliable. Naval bureaucrats in Washington and their field staff frequently suggested a vast array of alternative explanations. They claimed that error was inherent in submarine range estimates, that the agility of the Japanese in maneuvering their ships resulted in misses, and that U.S. submarine commanding officers exaggerated their claims under the fatigue of battle fire. However, evidence continued to mount to the contrary. For example, intelligence investigations

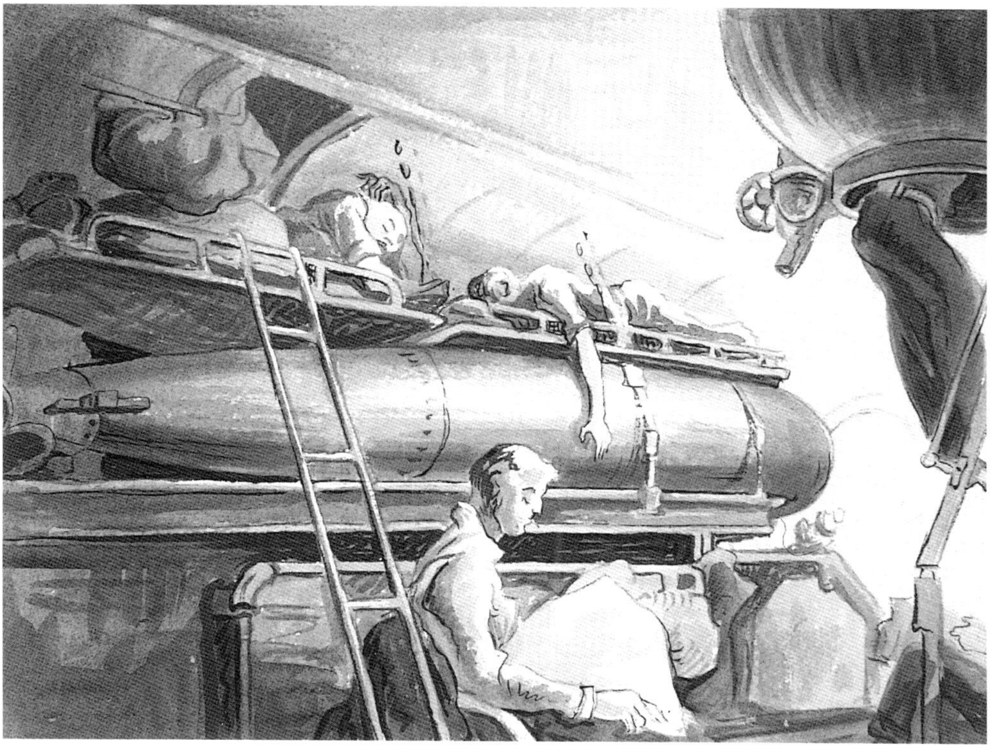

Above: *Slumber Deep* by American artist Thomas Hart Benton. (Courtesy of the Naval Historical Center 88-159-BK)

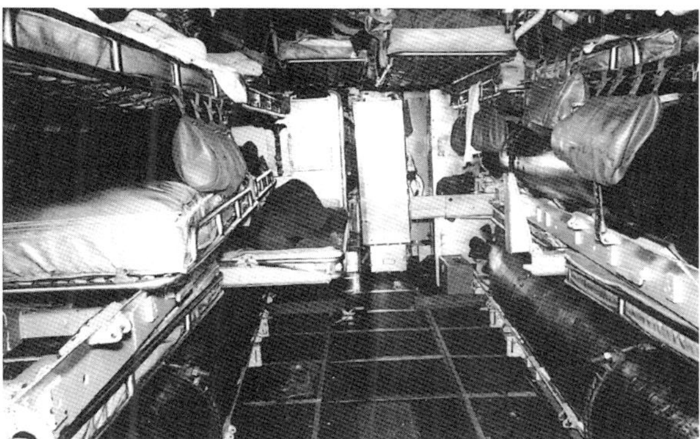

Right: The forward torpedo room, with six torpedo tubes, held eighteen torpedoes in this World War II-vintage American fleet submarine. The after torpedo room, with four tubes, held six torpedoes. (Photograph by the author)

discovered that the Germans experienced almost identical torpedo defects, which were not all corrected until December 1942. The British had also developed a magnetic exploder and abandoned it after it proved to be unreliable. On the other hand, Japanese torpedoes were the best in the world. Finally, after nearly twenty months of combat in the Pacific, the several complex problems that had plagued the manufacture of United States Navy torpedoes were solved. American submariners were relieved to have one less enemy to struggle with—their own torpedoes!

Several months before, however, in early 1943, OP-20-G finally agreed to cooperate fully with the silent service. Naval intelligence authorities in Washington concluded that the potential of submarines using ULTRA to direct their attacks far outweighed the risk of compromising the secret of Anglo-American cryptologic achievements. By this point additional Japanese codes as well as the grid system for their shipping operating areas had been solved. Convoys could be tracked at will. Submarines could sail to a crucial grid square to await the enemy's arrival rather than trying to catch sometimes fast enemy targets in long, high-speed chases. A special code readable only by submariners was designed by naval cryptographers. A submarine's coded messages, if intercepted by friendly surface ships, would appear to them as mere gibberish. Thus, ULTRA messages were given directly to the commander, Submarine Force, Pacific (ComSubPac), who used the special submarine code to send the highly secret information to submarines on distant patrol. This was done over the Pearl Harbor Fox net broadcasts. All submarines observed strict radio silence and they monitored the Fox traffic until their individual coded call sign appeared. They then copied and decoded their own messages. Only the commanding and executive officers and specially cleared radio operators had access to the "eyes only" ULTRA messages.

From January to October 1943, ComSubPac sent more than eight hundred ULTRA messages to submarines on patrol, that is, two or three per day. ULTRA led to the sinking of about half of all Japanese merchantmen claimed by American submarines. More reliable torpedoes also contributed significantly to Japanese merchant shipping losses during the war. Losses in gross tons reportedly were as high as 48,574 in December 1941; 884,928 in 1942; 1,668,086 in 1943; 3,694,026 in 1944; and 1,722,508 from January through August 1945. In comparison, however, German U-boats were by far the greatest antagonists of the supply operations during World War II. In the North Atlantic alone, excluding other areas in the Atlantic and the Indian Ocean where many U-boats operated, more than 23 million tons of merchant shipping was sunk. □

III

BACKGROUND OF UNITED STATES NAVY CARRIERS

No naval surface ship has had a more revolutionary impact on command of the sea than has the aircraft carrier. The British, not the Americans or the Japanese, were the first to develop aircraft carriers that featured speed and wind-over-deck capabilities sufficient for launching planes. Although two carriers were completed before the end of World War I (HMS *Furious* [19,513 tons displacement] and HMS *Argus* [14,550 tons]), they saw no action. (The *Argus* of 1918 was the world's first carrier capable of launching and landing aircraft.) Following these two pioneering carriers and until the late 1930s, British carrier aviation centered on the 21,630-ton *Eagle* and the 10,850-ton *Hermes* of 1924, and HMS *Courageous* and *Glorious*. The latter two ships were rebuilt from 22,500-ton battlecruisers in 1928 and 1929. Each carried forty-eight planes. Only one additional carrier—HMS *Ark Royal* (22,000 tons displacement, 31 knots top speed, 60 aircraft capacity)—was available to the Royal Navy before Hitler's invasion of Poland and the beginning of World War II in September 1939. Thus, despite earlier experimental carriers, Britain took little interest in naval aviation until the threat of war became clearer with the rise of Nazi Germany. Six new carriers were laid down before 1940, and they greatly extended British air power at sea when they were commissioned later during the war. Nonetheless, the Royal Navy lost three carriers—*Courageous*, *Glorious*, and *Ark Royal*—before the United States' entry into the war in December 1941. The HMS *Argus* was used as a training carrier.

The Americans and the Japanese were deeply interested in aircraft carrier development, but they lagged far behind the British at the outset of the 1920s. However, the two navies on opposite sides of the Pacific Ocean profited from the vigorous pioneering efforts of the British. Unlike the British, the Americans and Japanese were not weighed down by excessive gradualism in carrier construction programs. They were innovative and willing to make bold decisions in design: their second generation of carriers, for example, was consistently three times larger than the first.

The navies of Japan and the United States viewed each other with obvious misgivings early in the 1920s, and they were keen to explore new avenues in quest of special advantage over the other. The growth of carrier aviation in the Pacific, like the development of long-range submarines, received much attention in the two navies. At the Washington Conference of 1921-1922, Britain, which already had a significant advantage in carriers, suggested that the two Pacific rim countries convert two of their capital ships, which otherwise were to be scrapped, into aircraft carriers. Not surprisingly, both the United States and Japan endorsed the idea.

The USS *Saratoga* (CV-3). (The Mariners' Museum PN 1159 C163)

The United States converted two battlecruisers, which became the *Lexington* (CV-2) and the *Saratoga* (CV-3) in 1927. With a top speed of 33 knots, these large fleet carriers (37,681 tons displacement) far outclassed the first United States Navy carrier, the *Langley* (CV-1), which was highly experimental and had a displacement of 13,900 tons and a top speed of only 15.5 knots. The *Lexington* class carrier remained the heaviest of United States Navy carriers until the *Midway* class was first commissioned in September 1945.

Japan's first carrier was the *Hōshō* (9,330 tons displacement—25 knots top speed) of 1922. This was the first aircraft carrier in the world to be designed and built from the keel up specifically as a carrier, but the Imperial Japanese Navy's capital ship conversions permitted in the Washington Treaty resulted in vessels that dwarfed the *Hōshō*. The *Akagi*, a former battlecruiser, was commissioned as a 33,821-ton, 31-knot aircraft carrier in 1927. After its modernization and reconstruction were completed in 1938, the *Akagi* had a displacement of 40,650. Work to convert a second battlecruiser, the *Amagi*, was halted when the ship was wrecked on the stocks by the 1923 earthquake. The battleship *Kaga* was converted instead. Completed in 1928, the *Kaga* was about the same size as the original *Akagi*, but its top speed was nearly three knots slower. The Japanese navy, like the United States Navy, designed new carriers in the 1930s in light of experience, and by the time war broke out, the two navies were near parity in terms of naval aviation. Japan had nine carriers with a total capacity of about 549 aircraft and the

Above: Japanese light aircraft carrier *Hōshō*. (National Archives 351904)

Right: Looking forward at the anchor chain and capstan of the *Hōshō*. (National Archives 351903X)

Below: Postcard showing the fast heavy Japanese aircraft carrier *Akagi*. (The Mariners' Museum)

United States had eight carriers with a total capacity of about 578 aircraft. However, not all of the American carriers were in the Pacific when war started in December 1941.

Traditionally, the battleship was regarded as the final arbiter of naval battle, and fleet commanders frequently tied down and obligated the carriers to the role of flying patrols over the battleships and to supporting landing forces if amphibious operations were planned. Yet, in both the Japanese and American navies, maneuvers and war games were carried out, especially in the 1930s, that demonstrated the strike potential of air power if fast, highly mobile carriers were given freedom of movement from the battle line. Strategic geography in the vastness of the Pacific Ocean affected the American and Japanese conceptions of battle. It followed, therefore, that one particularly vital function, refueling at sea, became crucial if fast carriers were given freedom to make far-reaching air strikes. Refueling at sea was an intricate operation first successfully carried out in the United States Navy when the *Saratoga* refueled from a fleet oiler off California in June 1939. The first Japanese carrier to refuel while under way was the *Kaga* in September 1941.

Anchors Aweigh the Fast Carriers

Early in 1941, when various groups of Japanese military and economic expansionists advocated a push into Southeast Asia and the Dutch East Indies, Admiral Yamamoto, commander in chief of the Combined Fleet, was immediately mindful of the American battle fleet. The United States Navy decided in May 1940 to move the battleships previously based in San Diego to a new home port in Hawaii. Yamamoto feared that the United States Fleet at Pearl Harbor ("Pacific" was inserted into the fleet's title after February 1, 1941) would steam across the Pacific Ocean and attack his left flank. The American fleet was, after all, some 2,000 miles closer to the western Pacific, where the Japanese sought hegemony, than it had been while based at San Diego. Thus, the Philippines would be relieved by the American battleships, and Japanese lines of communication to the south would be interrupted. With this manifest dilemma before Japanese strategists, Yamamoto and his staff conceived of a fast carrier strike against the U.S. Pacific Fleet in Hawaii. The purpose was to sink the battleships and carriers alike, lest the latter fast ships strike in a clandestine manner against Japanese bases in an operation similar to that being planned against Pearl Harbor. After much debate and analysis, Yamamoto finally decided that the results expected from the air strike on Pearl Harbor would justify risking his irreplaceable fast carriers. However, total secrecy was of paramount importance.

The attack was masterfully executed in complete secrecy, and American forces were caught by surprise. American cryptologic agencies had made significant inroads into several Japanese secret communication systems, but in the late 1930s the Japanese made sweeping changes. In June 1939 the Japanese navy introduced a new code, called

JN25 by American cryptanalysts. OP-20-G had made limited progress in attacking this main Japanese operations code when a second, enlarged edition, JN25b, was introduced on December 4, 1941. Thus, when the attack came three days later, only about ten percent of the text of an average JN25b message could be read by American cryptographers. Moreover, when the six Japanese fast carriers sailed from Hitokappu Bay in the Kurile Islands en route to Pearl Harbor on November 26, complete radio silence was strictly observed throughout their approach to the Hawaiian Islands.

Top: The conclusion of the German-Italian-Japanese Tripartite Pact on September 27, 1940. Negotiations and telegraphic communications leading to this treaty, particularly between Berlin and Tokyo, helped United States Army cryptanalysts solve the Japanese Purple cipher system. Seen in this photograph from the left are Japanese Ambassador Saburō Kurusu, who was assigned to Germany for only a year, Italian Minister Count Galeazzo Ciano, Adolf Hitler, and German Foreign Minister Joachim von Ribbentrop. (From the author's collection)

Above: Hitler and Japanese Ambassador to Germany Hiroshi Ōshima, who arrived in Berlin in February 1941, were equally surprised by the news of the Japanese attack on Pearl Harbor. (National Archives 242-JRB-13-17)

The Japanese foreign ministry also changed its codes. In late 1938, the Japanese started to distribute a new cipher machine to their diplomatic missions that had previously used the Red machines. (The Red system had been compromised by the United States Army's SIS nearly five years earlier.) Given the name of a more intense color by American cryptanalysts, the new Japanese Purple machine was intended to be employed for the most secret of diplomatic communications. By the spring of 1939 the Purple machines were largely in place, and soon traffic in the less sophisticated Red system almost completely disappeared. The loss of Japanese diplomatic intelligence alarmed the American cryptologic community, and SIS, in particular, worked feverishly for the next eighteen months to discover the solution. Finally, Purple was broken in the latter part of 1940 while SIS studied the enormous flow of diplomatic traffic among the three Axis capitals—Berlin, Rome, and Tokyo—during negotiations leading to the conclusion of the tripartite military

This painting by John Hamilton shows planes flying off of Japanese aircraft carriers for Pearl Harbor, December 7, 1941. (Courtesy of the Naval Historical Center NHC AB 80-142-H)

pact of September 27, 1940. It was particularly noteworthy to American cryptanalysts that when the treaty was announced, the unclassified portions of the Axis pact were published in major newspapers around the world. During earlier Eurasian telegraphic negotiations, SIS was unable to read Japanese traffic; thus, the published text, with which SIS had been grappling for months, helped to provide the solution not only to the unclassified clauses of the treaty, but to the secret portions as well.

Privy though American cryptologists were to Japanese diplomatic traffic fourteen months later as the Imperial Navy's carriers sailed toward Pearl Harbor, Japanese diplomats at their posts around the world were not told about the navy's plans to attack the U.S. Pacific Fleet or anything about the execution of the plans. Total secrecy was observed. There was no reason for Japanese admirals to discuss their highly secret professional operations with civilian ambassadors. Thus, for example, the attack at Pearl Harbor caught Japanese Ambassador to Germany Hiroshi Ōshima, who was also an army lieutenant general on the reserve list, by the same degree of surprise that seized Americans in Hawaii. He first learned of the hostilities not long after Japanese carrier aircraft arrived over Oahu at 11:00 P.M. Berlin time on December 7, 1941.

Five Japanese midget submarines attempted to enter Pearl Harbor shortly before the start of the air strike on the morning of Sunday, December 7, 1941. This is a view of Ensign Kazuo Sakamaki's midget submarine that was wrecked on a reef near Bellows Field, Oahu, after it failed to reach the entrance to Pearl Harbor in December 1941. At Mare Island Naval Shipyard, California, in September 1942, President Roosevelt made one of several stops during a 9,000-mile trip around the country. As Secret Service agents stand guard, the president talks with Vice Admiral John W. Greenslade, commander Twelfth Naval District, and Rear Admiral Wilhelm L. Friedell, who commanded the shipyard at Mare Island. (Naval Historical Center NH 47036)

By April 1942, Japanese expansion was successful everywhere in the western Pacific, but at that point the Japanese navy's lack of a definitive strategic plan became critical, especially since the American aircraft carriers had not been caught like sitting ducks in Pearl Harbor four months earlier. Sweeping though Japanese expansion was, it had failed to reach a point where an effective defensive perimeter could be established.

Moreover, the Japanese realized there was no possibility of a negotiated peace with the United States as long as the United States Navy carriers were readily available for striking back. The "Doolittle Raid" on Tokyo and other Japanese cities on April 18, 1942, was an ominous sign of American tenacity and capability. The attack by Colonel James Doolittle's sixteen B-25 bombers was launched from the newly commissioned USS *Hornet* (CV-8) (19,875 tons displacement). Supported by the *Enterprise* (CV-6), four cruisers, and several destroyers, this group of ships, Task Force 16, was some 730 miles east of Tokyo when the strike was launched. Yamamoto thus believed that only an offensive naval strategy was suitable, at least in the short run, until a defensive perimeter could be established at greater distance from the heart of the Japanese Empire. Therefore, the decision was made to embark upon complex and highly coordinated operations —Operation "MI" for Midway, Operation "AL" for the Aleutians, and Operation "MO" for Port Moresby on the southeastern tip of New Guinea (Papua). More significantly, however, all three of these operations were scheduled to be carried out within roughly a thirty-day period.

The latter operation, Operation "MO," was the start of military undertakings intended to isolate Australia from the Allies by seizing the chains of islands running through the Solomons, the New Hebrides, and the Fijis to Samoa. Air bases on these islands would effectively extend reconnaissance searches and seal off Australia and New Zealand.

Control of the Coral Sea for purposes of neutralizing Queensland air bases was essential to the Japanese, but Allied intelligence used both traffic analysis and cryptologic intercepts to unmask Japanese intentions. Thus, Admiral Nimitz was able to make preparations. This sort of precision early in the war in the Pacific, before the

Sinking of the USS *Lexington* (CV-2) at the Battle of the Coral Sea, May 1942. (National Archives 80-G-16651)

American industrial capacity was at full tilt, was crucial to the United States Navy's survival. Nimitz's chief effort centered on the aircraft carriers *Lexington* and *Yorktown*, which moved into the Coral Sea approaches west of the New Hebrides on May 1, 1942. (The *Hornet* and *Enterprise* had taken part in the the Doolittle Raid and were not yet available.)

The ensuing Battle of the Coral Sea, concluding on May 8, was the first in naval history in which the ships of the two enemy forces never caught sight of each other; the entire action was fought by aircraft. The battle was probably a tactical victory for the Japanese, who lost the light carrier *Shōhō* (13,730 tons displacement); they also suffered heavy damage to the large carrier *Shōkaku* (29,330 tons displacement) and heavy losses in the *Zuikaku's* air group of experienced pilots. The United States Navy lost the *Sims* (DD-409), the fleet oiler *Neosho* (13,500 tons), and the fast carrier *Lexington*. Strategically, however, it was an American victory, in part because the important Japanese carriers *Shōkaku* and *Zuikaku* were unable to participate as planned in the Battle of Midway, less than a month away.

Indeed, Nimitz learned through cryptologic intelligence that trouble was brewing at Midway, some 4,000 nautical miles away from the Coral Sea. Therefore, he deliberately maneuvered defensively in the Coral Sea in anticipation of the next clash of the fast carriers.

As things became more focused and critical in the third week of May, Nimitz realized that he had little time to get his carriers into an optimum position for an ambush of the Japanese carrier strike force and still keep his extensive movements undetected. He had only three carriers available for the impending Battle of Midway. Intelligence revealed that the Japanese operation in the Aleutians was intended primarily as a diversion, with the hope that American forces would concentrate in the North Pacific and, therefore, be unable to defend Midway nearly 2,000 nautical miles to the south. However, Nimitz was aware that the Japanese engaged in radio deception. Those reports inevitably raised the terrible question of what was reality and what was merely deception.

Events were rapidly taking shape. The *Enterprise* and *Hornet* steamed into Pearl Harbor on May 26, about the same time Vice Admiral Chūichi Nagumo's four fast carriers—*Akagi, Kaga, Hiryū* (19,930 tons), and *Sōryū* (18,500 tons)—sortied for the 2,500-mile voyage from the Inland Sea of Japan en route to the vicinity of Midway. The *Yorktown* reached Pearl Harbor a day later from the Coral Sea, underwent emergency repairs in dry dock, and was out to sea again sixty-six hours later. The *Enterprise* and *Hornet* had sortied some forty hours earlier to make up Task Force 16 with five heavy cruisers, one light cruiser, and nine destroyers. Two heavy cruisers and five destroyers assembled around the carrier *Yorktown* made up Task Force 17.

The USS *Nautilus* (SS-168), August 3, 1943. (The Mariners' Museum LP 4798)

Left: Artist Frederic Freeman's depiction of the USS *Nautilus* (SS-168) sinking the Japanese carrier *Sōryū* at the Battle of Midway. In fact, the carrier was the much larger *Kaga* and only one torpedo from the *Nautilus* hit the carrier, but it failed to explode. (Courtesy of The Frederic W. Freeman Trust. Photograph by The Mariners' Museum, QW 0895)

Below: The listing USS *Yorktown* (CV-5) on June 7, 1942, after being torpedoed by the *I-168* the previous day. (The Mariners' Museum PU 168)

Above: The sinking of the USS *Yorktown* on the morning of June 7, 1942, as seen from an accompanying destroyer. The damage to the hull (visible at left) was caused by torpedoes from the *I-168* on the previous day. (Naval Historical Center NH 95575)

Right: The *I-68* completed at Kure Navy Yard on July 31, 1934, and seen here under way at 23 knots during its sea trials. Renamed *I-168* in May 1942, this submarine was responsible for sinking the already heavily damaged USS *Yorktown* at Midway in June 1942. (Naval Historical Center NH 73054)

At the time, Nimitz did not know the date of battle, but he was taking no chances. He wanted the carriers out of Pearl Harbor as soon as possible. And he wanted them as far out to sea and as close to the anticipated site of battle as possible, lest the Japanese spot them by flying boats or submarines. Much careful planning, hard work, good intelligence, and luck enabled the two task forces to rendezvous on June 2—well before the battle—in an ideal position northeast of Midway. They had considerable time to make final preparations for battle while waiting to launch surprise attacks on the Japanese carriers. With still more luck and careful direction on the American side, the Battle of Midway saw one of the most sophisticated employments of radio traffic and cryptologic intelligence in the war in the Pacific. Planes from the lurking American carriers struck with a vengeance on June 4; four barely suspecting Japanese carriers and their air groups were soon destroyed. Midway was a turning point in the naval war against Japan, and after the battle, cryptologic intelligence took the high road.

One American carrier was lost at Midway. At dawn on June 5, Admiral Nagumo sent two cruiser float planes to search eastward for the elusive United States Navy carriers. One of them found the *Yorktown* abandoned and drifting after heavy aerial attacks the previous day. The Japanese submarine *I-168*, already patrolling in the vicinity, was ordered to get the carrier. On the afternoon of the next day, the submarine skillfully penetrated the screen of destroyers around the wounded carrier while renewed rescue operations were being carried out by the destroyer *Hammann* (DD-412) alongside the *Yorktown*. Both ships were hit. The destroyer sank within a few minutes and the carrier finally turned turtle the next morning and sank. (This submarine attack was similar to the action of the USS *Nautilus* (SS-168) against the wounded Japanese carrier *Kaga* on June 4. However, the American submarine's torpedoes were not so effective; two missed and one struck amidships on the carrier but failed to explode.) In spite of heavy counterattacks by the *Yorktown's* destroyers, the *I-168* made good its escape.

Previous knowledge of the Japanese plans of battle gave Admiral Nimitz sufficient time to prepare his best possible defense. The tremendous distances of the Pacific theater saw U.S. naval forces, particularly the precious carriers, scattered over thousands of miles. Although Nimitz's decision to rush the carriers to an advantageous position northeast of Midway produced remarkable success, it was also daring, for if the Japanese struck elsewhere, American defenses, diverted to help support Midway Island, would probably have crumbled. It was only the beginning of a long war, but the American authorities who decided in the first half of 1942 to be prudently trusting of intelligence data became more sophisticated and competent in the fine art of wartime command, while the equally fine art of radio intelligence became more refined and mature.

The Sinking and Building of Carriers

The vital role of carriers in the war in the Pacific was unmistakable, and after Midway the competing navies stepped up efforts to replace their lost carriers and to increase carrier strength overall. Between the end of the arduous Battle of Midway and August 1945, fourteen Imperial Japanese Navy aircraft carriers were sunk, while the United States Navy lost eight. From 1941 to the war's end, construction of new carriers from keel laying until commissioning required on the average 12.9 months in American shipyards and 24.8 in Japanese shipyards. Fifty-four of these new carriers totaling 1,057,893 tons were commissioned in the United States Navy by August 1945. By comparison, eight new Japanese carriers were commissioned totaling 214,960 tons.

The strategy of converting various types of ships into carriers was pursued by both navies. Such conversions required on the average 8.5 months in the United States and 17.8 months in Japan. Forty-two converted carriers totaling approximately 568,812 tons were added to the United States Navy between 1941 and 1945. The Japanese converted nine ships into aircraft carriers during the same period; these carriers amounted to approximately 171,914 tons.

These statistics reveal not only the relative importance of aircraft carriers in the two navies, but also the decisive weakness of the Japanese shipbuilding industry throughout this protracted war of attrition. Moreover, work on several Japanese carriers was prolonged because of repeated aerial bombardments, and the vessels never reached commissioning before the war ended. In another case, work on the biggest carrier of the war, the *Shinano*, continued throughout the war until it was commissioned on November 19, 1944. Ten days later, however, only seventeen hours into its maiden voyage, the new leviathan was torpedoed and sunk by the American submarine *Archerfish* (SS-311). (The *Shinano* [62,000 tons] was not exceeded in standard displacement until the nuclear-powered USS *Enterprise* [CVN-65] was launched in 1960.)

Escort Carriers, ULTRA, and Antisubmarine Warfare

Many of the converted craft were classified as escort carriers in the United States Navy, and they sailed with and protected merchant convoys en route from North America to Great Britain and the Soviet Union. They also served as command ships in hunter-killer groups. Such a group typically included several destroyers organized around a 10,000-ton escort carrier for the specific purpose of hunting for enemy submarines. United States Navy hunter-killer groups were especially effective on the high seas when cryptologic intelligence was systematically integrated into antisubmarine warfare (ASW) operations.

The broader scope of the war at sea strained the effective operating ranges of several classes of U-boats, and arrangements for refueling at sea became necessary. U-tanker refueling operations were first carried out in April 1942 when the supply U-boat *U-459* met *U-108* some 500 miles northeast of Bermuda because surface tankers were being rapidly eliminated in the Atlantic. During the next two weeks the *U-459* refueled fourteen more combat U-boats in the same general area. Fourteen months later, by May 1943, more than four hundred U-boats were refueled by U-tankers. Each U-tanker had a reserve fuel capacity of 425 to 600 tons. Thus, the combat U-boat's effectiveness was easily doubled by extending its duration and range of operations. During the same fourteen-month period, U-boats sank on the average 561,192 tons of Allied shipping monthly, that is, 106.7 vessels. On the average, during the same period, slightly over twelve U-boats were sunk monthly. During the next fourteen months (June 1943–July 1944), on the average 136,870 tons of Allied merchant ships, or 26.2 vessels, were sunk monthly, while 20.8 U-boats were sunk monthly. The dramatic reduction of Allied losses and the increased destruction of U-boats were chiefly attributable to ULTRA and the introduction of hunter-killer operations with the intent of eradicating the U-tanker fleet.

Admiral Ernest J. King, commander in chief of the United States Fleet and chief of naval operations, pursued an aggressive ASW strategy by creating the Tenth Fleet on May 20, 1943. This new command had access to ULTRA, knowledge of the positions of all convoys and the availability of escorts, and the authority to issue sweeping orders without necessarily adhering to the traditional chain of command. The Tenth Fleet,

The USS *Bogue* (CVE-9). (The Mariners' Museum, Ted Stone Collection)

a shore activity with its headquarters in Washington, D.C., was responsible for all United States Navy ASW operations and control of shipping in the Atlantic, yet it was a fleet without a ship or an airplane specifically under its command. It was a think tank, an administrative fleet that offered great precision to ASW operations before its disbandment on June 15, 1945.

Four hunter-killer escort carrier groups, directed by Tenth Fleet headquarters, formed the spearhead of the ASW assault. They were built around the USS *Bogue* (CVE-9), the first and longest in Atlantic service; the USS *Santee* (CVE-29), which arrived in the Atlantic on June 13, 1943; the USS *Core* (CVE-13), in the Atlantic starting June 27, 1943; and the USS *Card* (CVE-11), which took up service in the Atlantic on July 30, 1943. Because of ULTRA specifically, planes from these four escort carriers sank twenty-four U-boats and one Japanese I-boat in the Atlantic by May 1945. (The Japanese submarine was engaged in east-west blockade-running Yanagi operations.) Four of these U-boats were U-tankers. Other U-boats were sunk with the aid of high frequency direction finding (HFDF) fixes. There were four additional escort carrier hunter-killer groups in the Atlantic. These were built around the USS *Block Island* (CVE-21), the USS *Guadalcanal* (CVE-60), the USS *Croatan* (CVE-25), and the USS *Wake Island* (CVE-65).

Above: Galley on the Japanese submarine *I-14*. (Naval Historical Center NR&L [M] 30936)

Right (top): The watertight door on the Japanese submarine *I-400*. This submarine was completed on December 30, 1944. The external surfaces of this class of submarine were covered with anechoic coating, an antisound-reflecting substance made of a resilient base of synthetic rubber and sand with a thin cement or plastic covering. The *I-400* class submarines were the largest submarines built by any nation prior to the close of World War II. They each had a displacement of 5,223 tons surfaced, 6,560 tons submerged. (Naval Historical Center NR&L [M] 30947)

Right: A view inside the hangar of the *I-400* where the Japanese crew is unloading supplies after surrender. Designed to carry three seaplanes, the giant *I-400* class submarine was intended for attack on the Panama Canal or ports along the Pacific coast of the continental United States. It was not surpassed in displacement until the United States Navy radar-picket submarine *Triton* (SSRN-586) was commissioned in November 1959. The Soviet "Hotel" class strategic nuclear submarines were also very large and nearly contemporary with the USS *Triton*. (Naval Historical Center NR&L [M] 30948)

Left: The Japanese crew unloading the *I-400* after surrender. The center tracks are for launching aircraft with a powerful catapult. (Naval Historical Center NR&L [M] 30937)

Below: The hangar door (left) and the bow of the *I-400* as the Japanese crew unload supplies after surrender. (Naval Historical Center NR&L [M] 30929)

Opposite (top): The after triple-mount 25-millimeter anti-aircraft guns aboard the *I-400*. (Naval Historical Center NR&L [M] 30941)

Opposite (bottom): The *I-14*, *I-401*, and *I-400* at Guam in November 1945 while en route from Japan to Pearl Harbor. (Naval Historical Center NMH 82107)

United States Navy Submarine Base with the escape training tower at Pearl Harbor in February 1946. In the foreground is the USS *Stickleback* (SS-415) with Japanese submarine *I-14* inboard of the American submarine and the *I-401* and *I-400* inboard of the *I-14*. (United States Navy, Ships and the Sea Collection 701060)

Quite logically, U-tankers became the focus of attack as ULTRA was used offensively for the first time. The target was at-sea refueling stations where U-tankers and combat U-boats awaiting replenishment fell prey to hunter-killer, radar-enhanced aerial attacks. By the end of the fourteen-month period (June 1943–July 1944), twelve U-tankers were sunk, as were 280 combat U-boats, many of them while rendezvousing with a U-tanker. Thus, the U-tanker fleet in the Atlantic was depleted and the whole U-boat campaign was severely undermined for the remaining nine months of war in Europe. U-boats were spending more time trying to survive ASW assaults than attacking Allied shipping. Two hundred forty-two additional U-boats were sunk by May 7, 1945, while only 167 Allied merchantmen totaling 758,797 tons were sunk—a far cry from the earlier U-boat records.

Escort carrier hunter-killer groups were used with similar efficiency late in the war in the Pacific, but their sweep of operations was much more limited than in the Atlantic. Nor was the Japanese submarine force as large or dominating as the German. One hundred twenty-seven of about 160 large Japanese submarines (I- and RO-boats) in service during the war were lost. (Comparable statistics on the German side of the Axis coalition suggest that 783 U-boats out of a force of 842 were lost.) Planes from the USS *Suwannee* (CVE-27) sank the Japanese submarine *I-184* east of Saipan in June 1944, but the most effective hunter-killer group in the Pacific was built around the USS *Anzio*

(CVE-57). The *Anzio* group sank the following Japanese submarines: the *I-41* east of Samar in November 1944, the *I-368* and *RO-43* off Iwo Jima in February 1945, the *I-361* east of Okinawa in May 1945, and the 3,703-ton *I-13* east of Honshū in July 1945.

The established United States Navy ASW strategy grew throughout World War II; the result was a sophisticated and imaginative foundation upon which more elaborate future ASW strategies were based. Although the Tenth Fleet was dissolved in 1945, its several components designed to produce greater precision in ASW operations—detection and location, classification and identification, and search and attack—remained in place. Moreover, naval planners recognized the need for a wide range of resources, including aircraft carriers, various types of destroyers, long-range land-based antisubmarine patrol aircraft, carrier-based fixed-wing aircraft, and a series of ancillary forces. However, intelligence remained the most significant component of effective ASW operations. Naval strategists knew that highly specialized equipment and weapons systems had to be closely coordinated with a hair-trigger intelligence system.

In spite of ASW operations, carriers played different roles in the Atlantic and the Pacific oceans. The fast aircraft carrier proved itself as the new capital ship, largely replacing the battleship in most Pacific battles. The American carrier became a principal means of naval assault. The aircraft carrier and the submarine together were indeed the chief means by which the Japanese navy was destroyed and the Empire's island territories were brought to surrender. Moreover, the development of naval air power and the submarine force was a function of the distinctive characteristics of the war in the Pacific—a war fought between two maritime nations directly struggling for command of the sea through carriers, codes, and the silent service. □

IV

IMPLICATIONS FOR THE NEW NAVY

Historians are often reluctant to venture into the future. Yet since our purpose in delineating certain developments in World War II is to make human beings wise forever about the nature of war, reflection beyond 1945 is essential. Otherwise, preparations for meeting some of the challenges of the twenty-first century might be poorly understood and inadequately supported by the public. On the other hand, professionals themselves do not have a clear view about what the future holds and how to prepare for it prudently. For example, in the first five issues in 1995 of the monthly forum for the sea services, the United States Naval Institute *Proceedings*, fifty-two of seventy feature articles addressed a vast array of post-Cold War tactical and strategic concerns. No thread of continuity or common theme emerged, although former Secretary of the Navy Sean O'Keefe sounded a note with which most of the authors would probably agree. Writing in the January issue, O'Keefe concluded that "[t]he world beyond our shores is unpredictable and dangerous, a place where we can [catch a] glimpse [of] the future only dimly." Within the more focused perimeters of carriers, codes, and the silent service, however, surely more explicit and meaningful assertions beyond World War II can be made. This will require us to build systematically on past experience and seek to understand conditions and requisites of the twenty-first century rather than seizing on high-tech hardware and formula-driven and futuristic issues that slip away in time like a handful of sand.

The Shroud of Intelligence

The urgency of World War II prompted Anglo-American cooperation in the field of cryptologic intelligence and eventually produced an unprecedented intelligence agreement. The broadening of the war in 1941 helped foster the new relationship. In particular, U-boat operations requiring United States Navy routing and rerouting of Atlantic convoys to Great Britain and the Soviet Union made British ULTRA-based intelligence extremely important. By 1942 the U.S. and Royal naval commands shared a considerable amount of cryptologic intelligence, and in October of that year the two navies concluded a formal agreement. Although it was limited and cautious and focused chiefly on U-boat Enigma traffic in the northern Atlantic, the agreement was an innovation that ran counter to the warning of earlier days that "today's comrades in arms could well be tomorrow's dangerous opponents."

The October 1942 naval agreement established a profound precedent. On May 17, 1943, the British War Office and the American War Department concluded a far more complex and wide-ranging cryptologic agreement, briefly referred to earlier. The five-page agreement between the War Department and the Government Code and Cipher School stated clearly that "both the U.S. and British agree to exchange completely all information concerning the detection, identification and interception of signals from, and the solution of codes and ciphers used by the Military and Air forces of the Axis powers, including secret services (Abwehr)."

The USS *Pickerel* (SS-524) with its raised head valve snorkel air intake, and the engine exhaust, below the deflection plate, which diffused the exhaust into the sea. Ten years into the Cold War, the *Pickerel* could easily remain on secret patrol for some thirty days while snorkling at night and charging batteries for remaining totally submerged during daylight. (Photograph by the author)

The Anglo-American partnership continued after the war, aided by various factors. Among them were the great increase of U.S. power on the international scene, the comparative weakening of Great Britain, and the increasing significance of Soviet strength. During the war years Churchill and Roosevelt had promoted cooperation between their respective intelligence communities. While Clement Attlee, who succeeded Churchill as prime minister in July 1945, exerted very little influence on Anglo-American secret relations, Harry Truman, the new American president after Roosevelt's death in April 1945, was generally in favor of postwar continuation of the British and American secret special relationship.

The president's top advisers started to consider how to adapt Anglo-American wartime intelligence machinery to conditions in the unsettling postwar world. The urgency of the Cold War intensified their efforts. Secretary of the Navy James Forrestal sent a letter dated May 23, 1945, to the commanding officer of OP-20-G at the Naval Communications Annex in Washington, D.C. (The day before, Forrestal had inspected OP-20-G, the navy's cryptanalytic center.) The secretary wrote that he "was greatly impressed . . . with the visit . . . [and] spoke of it to the President this morning and recommended to him very strongly that he make a similar visit himself, which he said he would do in the very near future." In September 1945 United States Army Chief of Staff George C. Marshall and Chief of Naval Operations Ernest J. King wrote a joint letter to Forrestal and Secretary of War Henry L. Stimson. They observed that

> [d]uring the German and Japanese Wars, the United States Army and Navy and the British Government Code and Cipher School collaborated closely . . . and exchanged fully the intelligence derived from cryptanalysis. The information resulting from this collaboration and exchange was an important factor in the success of many military and naval operations of the Allies.

Later in the month Secretary of State James Byrnes and the secretaries of War and the Navy sent a similar letter to the president, and Truman very soon issued a top-secret order to Forrestal and Stimson to continue, expand, modify, or discontinue cryptologic collaboration with the British, as determined in the best interests of the United States.

A thoroughly cooperative Anglo-American cryptologic arrangement was cemented into place, and coordination of intelligence activities increased as struggle with the Soviet Union worsened and Cold War animosity hardened. No real consideration was given to the idea of discontinuing the relationship; however, the British were obligated to assure the United States that they would not use secret information obtained from the collaborative arrangement to forward the international commercial interests of British business. The full-blown intelligence agreement was signed in 1948. In modified forms it very effectively served the interests of the United States and Great Britain throughout the Cold War, and has continued to the present. No doubt the Cold War arrangement was a legacy of the Anglo-American World War II collaboration against the Axis powers; together these arrangements from World War II and the Cold War form a solid backdrop for the work of the two intelligence communities as they look toward the far horizon of the twenty-first century.

Careful and thoroughgoing surveillance and analysis of potential turbulent regions of the globe are the hallmarks of these intelligence communities, which have broadened their membership to include various countries in the British Commonwealth of Nations and the North Atlantic Treaty Organization (NATO). Of course, not all tactical or strategic intelligence is continuously shared among the member states. Indeed, exchanges are sometimes intermittent, partial, selective, or dispensed with totally, depending on interests and circumstances. Yet the mission is preemptive: it is to detect challenges to international stability early so that diplomacy and economic persuasion, for example, can be given free rein before military force is threatened or actually used. When everything else has failed, if the application of military force is deemed necessary, reliable intelligence—for example, from signals, voice communications, satellites, and even secret agents—should enable commanders to be flexible, measured, and accurate in their undertakings. To be anything less is to court disaster.

The Depths of Silent Ships

The pattern of United States Navy submarine patrols, so wide-ranging and effective during the Cold War, received its baptism by fire in World War II, especially after ULTRA was fully integrated into submarine operations in 1943. What began as an adventuresome means of carrying the war to Japanese home waters starting shortly after the attack on Pearl Harbor became very elaborate and sophisticated operations by the summer of 1945. The operations were so successful, in fact, that there were virtually no Japanese ships left that were considered large enough to justify using an expensive torpedo to sink. Thus, largely antiquated submarine deck guns had their last hurrah by sinking of a lot of sampans. ComSubPac Vice Admiral Charles A. Lockwood wrote a top-secret report in 1947 on the value of ULTRA in the war against the Japanese. He noted that

> [i]n early 1945 it was learned from a Japanese prisoner-of-war that it was a common saying in Singapore that you could walk from that port to Japan on American [submarine] periscopes. This feeling among the Japanese was undoubtedly created, not by the great number of submarines on patrol, but rather by the fact, thanks to Communication Intelligence, the submarines were always at the same place as Japanese ships.

By the early 1950s the former offensive submarine patrol pattern was modified into a highly credible surveillance patrol system. From that time onward, there was hardly a day when American submarines were not lurking stealthily from strategic positions, particularly off the coasts of the Soviet Union or Russia. Submarine surveillance missions are likely to become even more important in the unstable post-Cold War era.

Advances in submarine technology and weapon systems increase opportunities for maintaining a promising and reliable capacity for defense and deterrence. In the September 1960 issue of *Saturday Review,* then Senator John F. Kennedy wrote that the

> Soviet acquisition of nuclear weapons and the means for their delivery anywhere on the face of the planet now makes certain that a nuclear war would be a war of mutual devastation. The notion that the Free World can be protected simply by the threat of "massive retaliation" is no longer tenable.

Kennedy's proposed solution was to press on with more vigor and hope "to seek in negotiations with the Russians effective means of arms control. . . . [However, the

Russians] are not going to take arms control negotiations seriously unless they are convinced that we shall soon have an invulnerable, mobile deterrent."

The United States Navy developed various missile systems, for example, the Regulus I system, before a nuclear-powered, cruise-missile strategic submarine was available. The navy sometimes employed clumsy, stopgap diesel-electric submarines as launching pads. Nor were the first nuclear-powered missile submarines altogether satisfactory. The USS *Halibut* (SSGN-587) was laid down in April 1957 and completed in January 1960. (U.S. strategic planners hoped that a submarine-borne missile would evade Russian defenses altogether because of the stealth of its carrier and launching

Left: The submarine *Pickerel* (SS-524) leaving the entrance to Tokyo Bay en route to a distant Cold War secret patrol area. (From the author's collection)

Below: The USS *Pickerel* in dry dock in Yokosuka, Japan. In preparation for making a secret patrol, workmen painted over the *Pickerel*'s hull numbers on the conning tower and on the bow shortly before this photograph was taken in February 1957. (Photograph by the author)

Above: The Japanese submarine *Oyashio* (SS-511) was the first submarine built in Japan after World War II. Completed in June 1960, this conservatively designed diesel-electric submarine had a submerged displacement of 1,420 tons, a surface speed of 13 knots (19 knots submerged), and a range of 10,000 nautical miles at 10 knots. The *Oyashio* was discarded from the Japanese Maritime Self-Defense Force in September 1976. (From the author's collection)

Right: One of the clumsy, stopgap diesel-electric submarines, the USS *Grayback* (SSG-574), halfway down the ways, was completed as a Regulus submarine in May 1958 and decommissioned six years later when Regulus was retired. However, the *Grayback* was brought back into service and converted to an amphibious transport (LPSS) in the late 1960s. (Official United States Navy photograph)

platform.) However, the *Halibut* was the only submarine of its class. Polaris missiles replaced the Regulus, and the *George Washington* and *Ethan Allen* (1960-61) classes of strategic submarines replaced the *Halibut.* And so the expensive progression continued throughout the Cold War. Ever more costly missile systems—the Poseidon (1968) to the Trident (1972) in several variants—were followed by ever more costly ballistic missile submarines to carry them. The first of thirty-one submarines of the *Lafayette* class (8,251 tons submerged) was completed in 1963 and the first of eighteen (built or being built) of the *Ohio* class (18,700 tons submerged) was completed in 1981. The last submarine of this class, USS *Louisiana* (SSBN-743), is scheduled for commissioning in late 1997.

Above: A Regulus I missile was launched from the USS *Halibut* (SSGN-587) on March 25, 1960. This marked the first firing of a missile of any type from a nuclear-powered submarine, although numerous missiles had been launched earlier from diesel-electric submarines. The Russians were also test-firing missiles from the "Hotel" class submarine in the early 1960s. (The Mariners' Museum, Ted Stone Collection USN K24757)

Left: The USS *Henry Clay* (SSBN-625) demonstrated for the first time on April 20, 1964, that a Polaris missile could be launched from a submarine on the surface. (The Mariners' Museum, Ted Stone Collection USN 1094722)

The USS *George Washington* (SSBN-598) sailing out of Pearl Harbor. (The Mariners' Museum, Ted Stone Collection)

However, the U.S. strategic submarine force has been reduced. All of the *Lafayette* and earlier classes have been eliminated; only the *Ohio* class remains, although some eighty-three attack submarines remain in service (to be reduced to forty-five to fifty-five boats by 2000). The reductions in numbers of strategic submarines, missiles, and warheads aboard the missiles finally came about because of successful negotiations with the former Soviet Union, because of the subsequent collapse of the Soviet Union, and later because of discussions with Russia and other autonomous parts of the former Soviet Union.

United States Navy post-1945 attack submarines underwent a series of often innovative modifications before the world's first nuclear-powered warship, the attack submarine USS *Nautilus* (SSN-571), was completed in April 1955. The snorkel and high submerged speed (19 knots in limited bursts) were prerequisites to seventy-nine submarines of the converted World War II Fleet Snorkel types and of four different types of Guppy submarines. Much experimentation was carried out with these submarines. For example, the USS *Pickerel* (SS-524) was completed as a Guppy II in 1949 and redesigned as a Guppy III in 1962 before being transferred to Italy in 1972. Ten other diesel-electric attack submarines made up three additional classes in the early 1950s (*Barracuda*, *Tang*,

Top: The USS *Permit* (SSN-594) leaving San Francisco Bay under the Golden Gate Bridge. (The Mariners' Museum, Ted Stone Co lection)

Above: The USS *Memphis* (SSN-691) was completed in December 1977 as an early *Los Angeles* class attack submarine. However, submarines of the improved *Los Angeles* class, starting with the USS *San Juan* (SSN-751), are twice as effective as earlier submarines of this class. (Official United States Navy photograph)

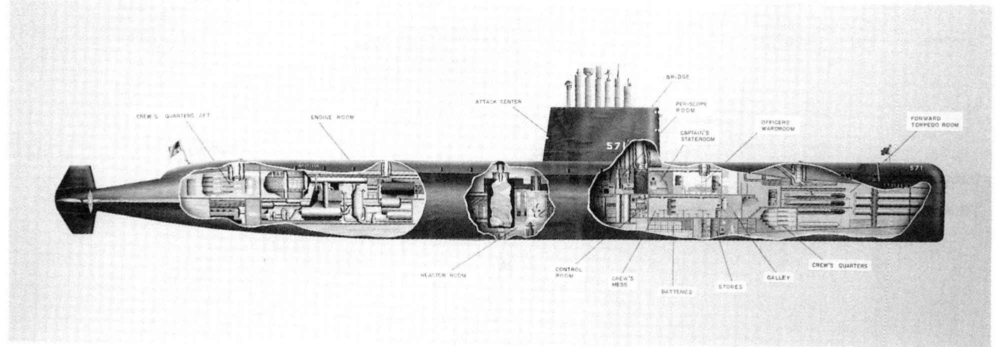

Top: Horizontal section of the USS *Nautilus* (SSN-571). (The Mariners' Museum QW 895)

Above: The USS *Nautilus* crash-surfacing on August 2, 1955. (National Archives 80-G-681184)

and *Darter* classes), but they were of little consequence before the *Nautilus*. Several other classes of attack submarines followed before the first of the *Los Angeles* class (SSN-688) was completed in 1976 at a cost of $225 million.

The next generation of United States Navy attack submarines is being introduced by the USS *Seawolf* (SSN-21). Nearly 2,000 tons heavier than the *Los Angeles* class and with twice the number of torpedoes, this super-quiet submarine is probably too expensive for the defense budgets of the 1990s. Nevertheless, after much delay and many cost overruns, the first boat of the *Seawolf* class is scheduled for delivery by late 1996, the second, USS *Connecticut* (SSN-22), is scheduled for 1998, and the third *Seawolf* is included in the FY 1996-97 budget, though debate about its fate continues.

Left: The USS *Bergall* (SSN-667) conducting an emergency surface test in September 1969. (National Archives K-77428)

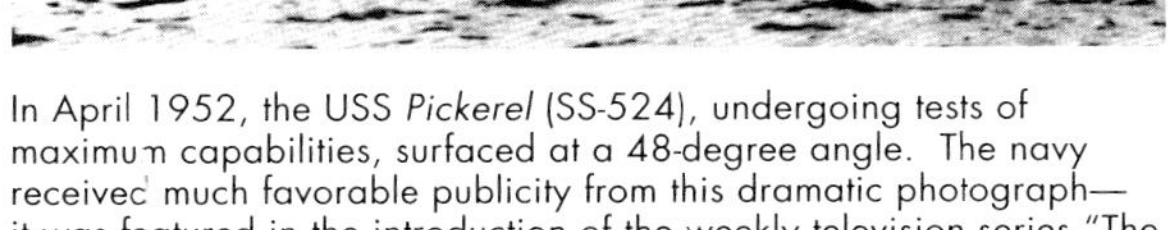

In April 1952, the USS *Pickerel* (SS-524), undergoing tests of maximum capabilities, surfaced at a 48-degree angle. The navy received much favorable publicity from this dramatic photograph—it was featured in the introduction of the weekly television series "The Big Picture" in the 1950s and early 1960s. (From the author's collection)

Top: Christmas dinner in the crew's mess during one of the *Pickerel*'s Cold War secret patrols. (Photograph by the author)

Above: Looking forward from the crew's mess into the control room of the USS *Pickerel*. (Photograph by the author)

Above: The USS *Wahoo* (SS-565) at Pearl Harbor. The *Tang* class, to which the *Wahoo* belonged, was the U.S. counterpart, initially, to the Soviet "Whiskey" class attack submarine, and, slightly later, to the Soviet "Zulu" class. Completed in 1951 and 1952, the six submarines of the *Tang* class attempted to assimilate various concepts from the German Type XXI U-boat. (Photograph by the author)

Yet the United States Navy seeks more funding for a post-*Seawolf* craft, a class of new attack submarines (NSSNs) estimated to cost $1.5 billion each. It wants to begin building in 1998 because the new multi-mission Russian submarine *Severodvinsk*, laid down in December 1993, is scheduled to become operational by 2000. By that year the navy estimates that 20 percent of Russian nuclear-powered attack submarines will be quieter than the USS *Toledo* (SSN-769), commissioned on February 24, 1995, the latest of the improved *Los Angeles* class. The last of the class, the USS *Cheyenne* (SSN-773), was launched in April 1995 and is scheduled to enter service in August 1996. Its cost will be at least $782 million, more than three times the cost of earlier submarines of the same class. But how big a margin of absolute superiority is necessary for safeguarding the legitimate interests of the United States?

The rhetoric of defense estimates notwithstanding, the chief problem with which the U.S. submarine force is likely to be confronted in the first few decades of the twenty-first century is not the Russian *Severodvinsk* class submarine. Rather, the greater difficulty will arise from the mass proliferation of submarine technology, most of it diesel-electric rather than nuclear-powered. Today five countries operate nuclear-powered submarines: Russia, with about 122; the United States, with some 97; Great Britain, with 15; and France and China, with about 9 each. No additional nuclear submarine forces

The USS *Enterprise* undergoing tactical maneuvers during the ship's shakedown cruise in October 1962. (The Mariners' Museum, Ted Stone Collection USN 1059657)

are expected to appear before 2010 or so. However, in addition to the 252 nuclear-powered submarines cited above, there are more than 350 diesel-electric submarines operated by nearly forty countries. These are highly affordable submarines available to Third World navies which, at least in some cases, are relatively proficient in submarine warfare. Traditionally, the Russian "Kilo" class submarine and the German *Type 209* boat have been popular purchases for these navies. Yet even more advanced, very quiet submarines are becoming available, for example, the Australian *Collins*, the Dutch *Walrus*, the British *Upholder*, and the German *Type 212* scheduled to enter service in 2003.

The threat to international stability appears increasingly grave as we move toward the twenty-first century. Modern, quiet diesel-electric submarines are difficult targets, and they operate most effectively in shallow water and at choke points in strategic waterways where they can stealthily lay deadly mines.

More extensive use of a lower-cost *Seawolf* alternative is a plausible course for navy strategic planners to pursue. With the end of the Cold War the world has become more, rather than less, unstable. However, the many potential disruptive forces in the world are technologically *inferior* to the United States, and the aggressors' purchase of modern foreign diesel-electric submarines will not give them a significant margin of naval strength unless such forces also enjoy the element of surprise. Thus, timely control of the sea, reinforced with strong intelligence and the surgically precise use of

The USS *Dwight D. Eisenhower* during sea trials in August 1977.
(The Mariners' Museum, Ted Stone Collection USN 1170823)

power, can best be managed by a sizable force of modern, thoroughly adequate attack submarines. The *crème de la crème* of submarine technology is too costly, and inarguably there will be too few of the *Seawolfs* and new attack submarines (NSSNs) to deal efficiently with numerous multidimensional international crises in the foreseeable future. Since it is likely that U.S. submarine force will be demanded in such crises, a practicable course for the United States Navy to pursue is the development of a non-nuclear submarine component to its undersea fleet. The conventionally powered *Barbel* class attack submarine, if reintroduced, would be an effective *Seawolf* complement. The last of the *Barbel* class, the USS *Blueback* (SS-581), was decommissioned on June 30, 1990. Highly sophisticated with updated technologies but obtainable at a lower cost, the new *Barbel* class would provide the United States Navy with a mix of non-nuclear and nuclear submarines that would allow it to approach future projections of power with measured force and surgical precision.

The Flight of the Imaginative Carrier Force

The big aircraft carriers that were allowed the Japanese and American navies at the conclusion of the Washington Conference in 1922 proved to be pivotal to fast carrier operations in World War II. Converted from battleships or battlecruisers, the Japanese and American chief treaty carriers—*Akagi*, *Kaga*, *Lexington*, and *Saratoga*—had an average displacement of 35,586 tons and an average top speed of 31.2 knots. Their aircraft complement was about sixty-one planes each. These physical characteristics, modified upward as a result of modernization work before the war, were drawn upon extensively during fleet maneuvers in the 1930s and later in the war in the Pacific, where vast distances figured prominently in naval operations. Vice Admiral Chūichi Nagumo's fast carriers, for example, completed extensive operations during the first four months of the war between Hawaii and Ceylon, a distance of one-third of the way around the world. The carrier task force proved to be an effective way to project power with speed and precision during World War II, and it is not surprising that during the Cold War the need for sea-based aviation was met by the same basic vehicle, the fast carrier task force.

The size and capability of United States Navy carriers have grown tremendously since the Japanese surrender in 1945. The initial ship of the *Midway* class was commissioned at the same time, and was the first American carrier to exceed the size and capabilities of the *Lexington* class of 1927. The *Midway*'s displacement was greater by nearly 10,000 tons, it had a greater complement by some eighteen hundred sailors, and it carried twice as many aircraft as the *Lexington*. The *Forrestal* class (1955) was still larger, and was the first carrier designed to operate jet aircraft. The *Enterprise* (CVN-65), commissioned six years later, was the first with nuclear propulsion. Since the commissioning of the *Nimitz* in 1975, all United States Navy carriers constructed have been nuclear-powered. The *Nimitz* class of carrier has completely dominated American carrier-building since. After the *Nimitz* (CVN-68) came the *Dwight D. Eisenhower* (CVN-69) in 1977, the *Carl Vinson* (CVN-70) in 1982, then *Theodore Roosevelt* (CVN-71), then *Abraham Lincoln* (CVN-72), then *George Washington* (CVN-73), which entered service in 1992. The *John C. Stennis* (CVN-74) is scheduled to be completed in late 1995, the *Harry S. Truman* (CVN-75) is scheduled for mid-1998, and the *Ronald Reagan* (CVN-76) will appear in service near the turn of the century.

There is no doubt about the ability of present-day carrier task forces to react in a crisis. In early 1991, in response to the Iraqi invasion of Kuwait, the *Theodore Roosevelt* was ordered to the scene. Steaming day after day at speeds considerably in excess of 35 knots, the 96,000-ton, two-reactor supercarrier was the most formidable manifestation of U.S. combat strength to reach the area at the outset. In Desert Storm and throughout the Cold War, and in the Korean and Vietnam wars, for example, American carrier task forces have acquitted themselves very well. They have met with virtually no opposition in the last fifty years—certainly nothing comparable to the onslaught of Japanese kamikaze and conventional air attacks or deadly Japanese submarine torpedoes.

Modern, efficiently manned, well-maintained, and well-equipped carrier battle groups are neither subtle nor inexpensive. Their state-of-the-art technology is thoroughly reliable. They utilize for defense the cutting edge of futuristic technology. They were ideal instruments for the Cold War strategy of destroying the economy of the Soviet Union even at the risk of jeopardizing our own. But to maintain twelve carrier battle groups is

An overhead view of the Sixth Fleet Task Force 60 ships steaming in formation in the Mediterranean Sea in March 1976. The two aircraft carriers are the USS *Saratoga* (CV-60) and the USS *Independence* (CV-62). (The Mariners' Museum, Ted Stone Collection USN 1167160)

arguably no longer an affordable, infallible contingency plan for the twenty-first century, when United States foreign policy ambitions must be more refined than they have been to date in the 1990s. More is needed from the most imaginative American military strategists in order to protect reasonable U.S. concerns. American society has a right to expect genuinely new ideas to meet the challenges of a new era. U.S. policy at the outset of the next century should not be wedded to the dreadnought-like mentality that governed U.S. naval policy at the outset of this century.

Today, in the aftermath of the Cold War with its staggeringly costly arms race, and in the foreseeable future, the United States Navy is the most powerful fleet in the world. Judicious down-sizing, as contemporary naval parlance would have it, is essential because a strong naval adversary is not likely to materialize, and the public increasingly questions the cost of maintaining an exaggerated naval presence around the globe. Adaptability and agility—not bigness per se—will be the watchwords in the prudent application of naval force. Precision and refinement of weapon systems, promoted by intelligence, are chief goals since the public has grown less and less willing after World War II to accept heavy casualties. □

Selected Bibliography of Works in Print

Boyd, Carl. *Hitler's Japanese Confidant: General Ōshima Hiroshi and MAGIC Intelligence, 1941-1945.* Lawrence: University Press of Kansas, 1993.

——— and Akihiko Yoshida. *The Japanese Submarine Force and World War II.* Annapolis, Md.: Naval Institute Press, 1995.

Drea, Edward J. *MacArthur's ULTRA: Codebreaking and the War against Japan, 1942-1945.* Lawrence: University Press of Kansas, 1992.

Dull, Paul S. *A Battle History of the Imperial Japanese Navy, 1941-1945.* Annapolis, Md.: Naval Institute Press, 1978.

Dupuy, Trevor N. *Future Wars: The World's Most Dangerous Flashpoints.* New York: Warner Books, 1992.

Friedman, Norman. *U.S. Aircraft Carriers: An Illustrated Design History.* Annapolis, Md.: Naval Institute Press, 1983.

———. *U.S. Submarines through 1945: An Illustrated Design History.* Annapolis, Md.: Naval Institute Press, 1995.

———. *U.S. Submarines since 1945: An Illustrated Design History.* Annapolis, Md.: Naval Institute Press, 1994.

Fukui, Shizuo. *Japanese Naval Vessels at the End of World War II.* Annapolis, Md.: Naval Institute Press, 1992.

George, James L. *The U.S. Navy in the 1990s: Alternatives for Action.* Annapolis, Md.: Naval Institute Press, 1992.

Grove, Eric. *The Future of Sea Power.* Annapolis, Md.: Naval Institute Press, 1990.

Hickam, Jr., Homer H. *Torpedo Junction: U-Boat War off America's East Coast, 1942.* Annapolis, Md.: Naval Institute Press, 1989.

Jentschura, Hansgeorg, Dieter Jung, and Peter Mickel. *Warships of the Imperial Japanese Navy, 1869-1945.* Translated by Antony Preston and J. D. Brown. Annapolis, Md.: Naval Institute Press, 1976.

Kahn, David. *Seizing the Enigma: The Race to Break the German U-Boat Codes, 1939-1943.* Boston: Houghton Mifflin, 1991.

Kelshall, Gaylord T. M. *The U-Boat War in the Caribbean.* Annapolis, Md.: Naval Institute Press, 1994.

Kennedy, Paul. *Preparing for the Twenty-first Century.* New York: Vintage Books, 1993.

Miller, Edward S. *War Plan Orange: The U.S. Strategy to Defeat Japan, 1897-1945.* Annapolis, Md.: Naval Institute Press, 1991.

Palmer, Michael A. *Origins of the Maritime Strategy: The Development of American Naval Strategy, 1945-1955.* Annapolis, Md.: Naval Institute Press, 1990.

Parillo, Mark P. *The Japanese Merchant Marine in World War II.* Annapolis, Md.: Naval Institute Press, 1993.

Poolman, Kenneth. *Allied Escort Carriers.* Annapolis, Md.: Naval Institute Press, 1988.

Reynolds, Clark G. *The Fast Carriers: The Forging of an Air Navy.* Annapolis, Md.: Naval Institute Press, 1992.

Roscoe, Theodore. *United States Submarine Operations in World War II.* Annapolis, Md.: Naval Institute Press, 1949.

Silverstone, Paul. *U.S. Warships since 1945.* Annapolis, Md.: Naval Institute Press, 1987.

Sokolsky, Joel L. *Seapower in the Nuclear Age: The United States Navy and NATO, 1949-80.* Annapolis, Md.: Naval Institute Press, 1991.

Stern, Robert C. *The* Lexington-*class Carriers.* Annapolis, Md.: Naval Institute Press, 1993.

Winton, John. *ULTRA in the Pacific: How Breaking Japanese Codes & Ciphers Affected Naval Operations against Japan, 1941-45.* Annapolis, Md.: Naval Institute Press, 1994.

Y'Blood, William T. *The Little Giants: U.S. Escort Carriers against Japan.* Annapolis, Md.: Naval Institute Press, 1987.

Index